As a professional speaker, I found the language of business and negotiation tactics especially compelling. This book is a roadmap for mastering the art of persuasion.

Susmitta Dutta | Author, *Pivotal Leadership*

The intersection of faith and business in this book is refreshing. Funke and Absa remind us that belief systems are powerful tools that can strengthen, not complicate, our leadership journeys.

Dr. Michelle Wicmandy | Global Marketing Communications, KBC (A Yokogawa Company)

Funke and Absa beautifully weave nature's lessons into leadership principles that can transform communities. This is a must-read for anyone passionate about driving social change.

Tamara Nall | CEO & Founder, The Leading Niche

The analogies to natural ecosystems provide profound insights into human behavior and organizational dynamics. A must-read for those in leadership and team development.

Brandon Blewett | Best selling author, *How to Avoid Strangers on Airplanes*

Modern Leadership: Inspired by Mother Nature

The Women and Wisdom Series

FUNKÉ NNENNAYA MICHAELS
&
NDEYE ABSA GNINGUE

ISBN **978-1-63735-367-7** (pbk)
ISBN **978-1-63735-368-4** (hcv)
ISBN **978-1-63735-366-0** (ebook)

Library of Congress Control Number: **2024926703**

Dedication

The women of Africa have been leading since time began,
since the first woman learned to navigate
through the business of living.
To all the women who make our Earth vibrate
with the passion for life and business.
Kudos to you!

Table of contents

ACKNOWLEDGMENTS

We are grateful to the members of our respective families and to our work teams: the amazing people who make it possible to do business in real-time.

To the patient editorial team, we offer our profound thanks for the dexterity in managing two authors on three continents during this project.

We are equally grateful to each contributor, case study respondent, and collaborator for sharing personal insights and encouraging us throughout the writing process.

Foreword

In a world where the dynamics of leadership are constantly shifting, women are rising with a wealth of unique insights and untapped potential. As mothers, partners, and simple human beings, we navigate the complexities of modern leadership while often overlooking one of the most profound sources of wisdom: NATURE itself. She has been an extraordinary teacher and an infinite source of inspiration. She has helped us foster resilience, adaptability, and harmony—qualities that are essential for effective leadership.

This book, *The Women and Wisdom Series: Modern Leadership: Inspired by Mother Nature,* is not just a guide; it is a rallying call for women leaders everywhere. It invites us to transcend conventional frameworks and delve into the lessons that nature imparts as we forge strong, sustainable paths in leadership. Just as ecosystems thrive on diversity and balance, our leadership must embrace inclusivity and interconnectedness, celebrating the spirit of sisterhood.

I have always been passionate about sustainable development and women empowerment. I have used my scientific background to add value to our rich heritage that has been handed over to us by our elders.

Phytotherapy, medicinal plants, especially the indigenous ones in our region, and our unique biodiversity have all helped to forge my career pathway. I have always believed in operating at the intersection of science, environment, and leadership, and this is the reason why I believe that this book provides invaluable insights for any woman seeking to deepen her leadership journey. It offers a refreshing perspective on how aligning with nature can inspire authenticity, innovation, and a deeper connection to both ourselves and the world around us.

Within these pages, you will discover not only inspiration but also practical wisdom that empowers you to lead with purpose, resilience, and renewed balance. Let us embrace the lessons from Nature and weave them into our leadership journeys, creating a legacy of impact that will resonate for generations to come.

Ameenah Gurib-Fakim, PhD

President of the Republic of Mauritius (2015-2018)

Modern Leadership: Inspired by Mother Nature

The Women and Wisdom Series

FUNKÉ NNENNAYA MICHAELS
&
NDEYE ABSA GNINGUE

Preface

When Funké and I first discussed the Women and Wisdom Series, it began as a collection of sayings, proverbs, and life lessons gathered from our forebears. The idea was to develop an arsenal of wisdom from traditional communities, which would equip those women who are in leadership roles today or who are growing into such roles in the future. As an advisor and cultural reference on relevant traditional systems and shared wisdom, I have seen the concept grow to encompass the full gamut of professional and personal development guidelines applicable to several scenarios and useful for continuous learning in management.

Across Africa and other parts of the Global South, "wisdom management" is a generational tool typically passed down from parent (or grandparent) to child. The lessons learned turn out to be invaluable in handling real-life situations and in the day-to-day running of businesses. The socioeconomic benefits can be seen across the board: from vast urban concerns, which are female-run, to resilient rural market systems, which are almost entirely dependent on the wisdom and ingenuity of our smallholder's female workforce. In many ways, the hand that rocks the cradle also props up the local economy.

Wisdom in the female sub-economy is further helped by underpinning the security of rotational savings in women's groups and their commitment to cross-invest by pumping pooled funds into one another's business, ensuring that members grow collectively as well as individually. Such co-operative entrepreneurship is often backed by experience-based advice from older group members. While avoiding common business pitfalls or receiving tips on work-life balance may seem like trivial reasons to gather, it often leads to greater gains, as shown in Michaels and Gnignue's work. For many, this socioeconomic gathering (like that of swarming butterflies) becomes a bedrock of mutual support and mentorship, which is accessible to each member of the community.

Thanks to digital technology, the traditional practice of rotational savings has been modernized and spread across several apps and platforms, with obvious financial gains. Our expectation is that with this work, the authors have begun a much-needed move towards making the often-forgotten aspects of shared wisdom available for application in today's setting. As practitioners, and teachers of management, it is important to increase the body of work in this sub-genre so that everyday people can access examples they can apply to their own lives and businesses.

This book brings together Michaels and Gningue's own experiences with careers that span five continents and several high-efficiency roles. With about 50 years of collective experience between them, their specific applications of lessons learned, the framing of Africa's unique market, the tips on how to surmount hurdles and navigate barriers created by the social construct, and the symbolic representation of Africa's exotic wildlife as emblems of wisdom, are all highlights that make this work relevant and relatable to all. By making it adaptable to models that prioritize teaching-over-time, the authors lay a foundation for "show-and-tell" opportunities where co-learning leads the readers or learners to spontaneous self-development.

During a recent conference session held in Florence, Italy, where the discourse centered around international partnerships and Artificial Intelligence in Sub-Saharan Africa, one attendee asked how it is that the numbers and usage opportunities from Africa show such positivity despite the challenges of working in that market. The answer is intuitive to most traditional Africans, raised to view the world through a lens of hope and trust in a better future with proverbs and sayings to address just about every challenge known to mankind.

For those who wonder how Africa's optimism permeates through the apparent difficulties faced, this book gives insight into the kind of strength and innovative thinking necessary for survival in the challenging and ever-changing landscape. The lessons from Mother Nature remind us all that answers have always existed in the flora and fauna that surround us. Michaels and Gningue remind us that, like our forebears who looked closely and learned from Nature, we can also find the understanding and courage for the long but adventure-filled road ahead.

Professor Abiola Awosika

Introduction

When most non-Africans think of the continent, it is usually in the context of natural resources, economics, socio-political alignments, or the effects of these on global business. Most of the data and insight on the African continent have been structured around countries and the economies of regions or sections. The geographical definitions of African economics cannot be ignored. Yet, we often neglect the most basic of Africa's definitions: the immediate community governed by a set of unwritten but accepted rules that affect every aspect of daily living—especially commerce.

To the traditional structure of African communities, modernity has added the more widely accepted norms and rules of engagement that translate to global markets. In order to get the average African entrepreneur to understand these rules of global business, we must go back to the community and learn the language of the land. The fluidity of communities like the Abaluhya of Kenya and Uganda; the Touareg of Mali; the Fulani of Niger, Nigeria, Chad, Senegal, Gambia, and Guinea; as well as the Yoruba of Nigeria, Benin, Togo, and parts of Ghana, are a few examples of economies that are affected more by movement than by country borders. These micro-migrations affect trade, education, infrastructural capacity, and even election results in the region.

The traditional trade structures where communities attained mutual trust over several generations of business or artisanship have given way to modern entrepreneurship and mobile money, where transactions are instantaneous. Exchanges are based less on trust and more on the availability of funds to support continued trading. With most businesses, raw materials for production come from several sources. The local sources are often rural, with challenges in logistics and business infrastructure, while the foreign sources are often affected by exchange rate fluctuations, political instability, and the availability of ready cash for payments. In the absence of a credit system that bridges the local African business with suppliers and buyers on the global market, African entrepreneurs continue to use scarce resources to produce goods and provide services that are disadvantaged from the onset.

CHAPTER 1

Women: Thriving in a Man's World

By highlighting the major pain points of the personas reviewed in this book, we are able to distill viable solutions and learn from each scenario. We use real African business and leadership examples to reflect the peculiar challenges of our environment, in order to show how creative reasoning can help in surmounting both professional and personal challenges. Each example is a pointer to the relationship between Mother Nature and the required leadership character. For each animal, we outline five key learnings that are easy to remember and incorporate into everyday life.

This is an indigenous children's teaching model learned from our grandparents. Since there are five fingers on each hand, a learner can associate one key message with each finger, thus making it easier to remember all five points. It also discourages lesson overloading by making it easier to understand how these simple principles have served other women in leadership roles.

A. Work with Wisdom

It took a few years before I noticed the title change. My staff had gone from calling me "Madam" to "Oga-Madam" even in my absence. Oga, being a word reserved strictly for leading males in our patriarchal Nigerian society, I was very proud to have arrived at that title. The new prefix was a subtle acknowledgement that I had earned the right to be called Boss. It was taken for granted that in the African sense of female management, I rose through the ranks to reach my current role. It was well understood that I could be the boss without necessarily "bossing" anyone around. The double title was a sign of deference that came with time spent on the same team and trust earned from working on several projects together—with shared stress and sacrifice.

Like many female colleagues working in majority male-led organizations, finding a balance between leadership and friendship in a professional sense became necessary. To foster the kind of loyalty that bonds a team together while maintaining the formality of work relationships, I needed to learn from women who had done it before me. There was a willingness to form communities of like minds in similar situations where women leaders could learn from one another. From workplace savings and housing schemes to handholding through career advice and referrals, women in the marketing eco-system found it easier to do business when there were more of us on the table. Standing up and speaking up in the face of cultural stereotypes, female managers began to mentor other females into positions of higher responsibility, with impressive outcomes. In the course of my career growth, I was fortunate to cross paths with many such positive females.

B. Be Gentle, Be Firm

There is a common misconception that females in leadership positions must be tough, especially in male-dominated work environments. The need to maintain professional distance can be made more isolating when added to the pre-conceived stereotypes that surround women in the workplace. There are subtle ways in which attitudes differ when it comes to women in leadership roles. For many reasons, the concept of work is different for females in most African settings, and the choices that society presents to female managers are sometimes vastly divergent compared to their male counterparts.

Women leaders have had to hone their skills and then have the humility of winning gracefully when their good work pays off. Earlier in my career, I had the privilege of working as part of a creative advertising team. I was the youngest member of the team of which the only other female was our office secretary. The influence of culture on the work environment was such that it was easy to co-exist as members of one family, with the attendant terms of respect and endearment. I learned to address the older graphic artists as my big brothers, and rather than give instructions, I learned to ask them what they thought and how they thought it would best be expressed. It was easier to achieve consensus that way, and it created a friendlier platform for giving constructive feedback when things did not go as planned.

This gave the relationship a less serious framing and allowed us to work well despite being of different ages, tribes, and cultures. The mutual respect that came from seeing one another as humans first became a key to managerial success in my later roles. The ability to find a non-threatening position of power thus became a defining factor in my work. Younger female managers learned to get good work done without needing to bully our direct reports. Teammates also learned to deal with a growing number of females in leadership roles where the usual cultural hurdles of age and gender did not apply.

As I grew in the industry, I began to find women like myself who are willing to support other women in their chosen careers and who are able to share what they have learned over the years. In one of the most serendipitous meetings of my own career, I got the chance to work with Ndeye Absa Gningue, an encounter that has led to many laudable projects, of which this book is but one outcome. Having somewhat similar outlooks, with backgrounds steeped in African wisdom, we see in one another the undeniable proof that wisdom does make a difference in managing high-octave careers with the demands of everyday life.

C. Be Strategic

In the chapters that follow, Absa and I use African analogies to explain the business values that have worked for us and other women. At the end of each chapter, we use simple visuals as reminders of our five-point lesson. Lastly, we include a fun activity that helps articulate your personal growth strategy better. Whether you are just starting on your growth journey or at a point where expansion or re-orientation is necessary, you will find wisdom here from leaders who have been in similar situations.

The aim of this project is to show that good leadership has the same profitable outcome, regardless of gender and culture. Humans will respond intuitively to positive stimuli, the same way consumers and communities react to positive market stimuli. As female leaders in corporate intrapreneurship and serial entrepreneurs, Absa and I bring our expertise with the intention of positively stimulating development within our economies through co-learning and mutual business support.

The African analogies show strategies that have proven useful for working women in today's fast-paced environment. We use Nature to frame the character of leadership that is necessary within our environment. The beautiful wildlife of Africa becomes a canvas on which the lessons in leadership are painted. Using traditional teaching methods with animals as symbols of strategic leadership, we aim to set easy reminders for readers to use in everyday business relations.

Regardless of age or gender, wisdom is profitable for all forms of leadership. Tailored to support deliberate, aspirational leadership—especially in females—we have arranged illustrations in this book to lead readers to measurable points of progress. At the end, when the reader has gone through all ten personas, they may choose the ones that best reflect their personality, unveiling a self-made map to personal growth. With physical facilitation activities, these elements are used to aggregate findings, fine-tune personal or business strategies, prepare realistic budgets, execute set plans, and measure individual growth from these co-learning exercises.

In the traditional African way, leadership learning begins before actual leadership responsibilities are given. Certain generational skills are passed down from lessons given in early childhood. This continuous line of co-learning has been the bedrock of our communities, with cooperation among traders and skilled groups. By the time an apprenticed learner takes the reins of a business, trust has been earned from the trainer, and years of experience have been given along with network support from third-party stakeholders. This explains why generational businesses survive based on historical pedigree and customers' trust in the continued existence of that business.

From our workplace experiences, we see that modern leadership first accepts performance potential as proof of future profitability and then trains the individual to meet or surpass that potential. In well-structured organizations, this training is laid out over a planned period of time, with promotions and incentives to encourage participation. On the corporate frontier, mentoring relationships take the place of apprenticeships, nonetheless achieving similar outcomes. Using the same principles of wisdom by adding historical advantage to technological ease, experienced leaders train new intakes by passing on the knowledge and trade tricks that are tried and trusted.

D. Learn Leadership Through the Line

I was 21 when I fell into the lap of advertising. I had just earned my bachelor's degree from the University of Benin and survived my first heartbreak. I believed I was truly on my way into adulthood. I walked into Centerspread as a novice, and by the time I left, I was indelibly marked and inarguably sold on what I wanted to do for a living. I watched the agency's executive director, Foluke Kamson, very carefully, noting the mix of stern professionalism with occasional revelations of her fun-loving alter ego. She excelled at keeping the teams on track, making sure we remembered that work had to be done and timelines had to be met.

"Ise wa o! There is work o!" Her half-teasing voice would be heard in the hall just off the reception door. It kept everyone on their toes without being overbearing. In the environment of Studio B, where I worked as a copywriter, we were building a work family with teammates invested in the progress of the work. We did that while having as much fun as legally allowed at the workplace.

The next 10 or so years were spent at different tables of the same party. I moved to STB McCann (STB McCann is an advertising agency in Nigeria that is part of the McCann Worldgroup network.), where I managed a healthy variety of brands across various industries. I had a particular admiration for the executive director, Nike Alabi's astute business mind. The beauty of working with female-led teams is that one gets to see comparable styles of leadership. I had the good fortune of working with Mimi Owodunni, Timi Deinsa-Adamolekun, Bolade Badmus, and Kehinde Bademosi, teammates who remain close industry allies to this day. Working at the corner of copywriting and client service, I had dotted-line reporting relationships with several other departments, giving me the opportunity to learn from each of those units as I grew. I got to have a well-rounded view of the advertising eco-system, and thanks to Ms. Alabi's ingenuity, I was seconded to Coca-Cola Nigeria as Advertising Liaison Manager.

Having met the brand in different ways my entire life, to be allowed into the sanctum of marketing on the world's number one brand meant that I had arrived. I went in with a sponge, absorbing as much as I could of the theory and practice of Brand Coca-Cola. Under the directorship of Abraham Ninan, I began to understand the business end of brand management. With the active mentorship of female-supporting men like Reuben Onwubiko, the late Ken Nwachukwu, Oare Ojeikere, Yinka Akande, and Sedi Inwutube, I made a full entry into marketing, finally understanding how my professional journey had brought me to that point in my career.

In the following years, I was lured to join the e-banking team at Fountain Trust Bank. Seeing the promise of a digital future, I jumped from core marketing into digital platform exploitation. I gathered experience on the financial side of the business, learning the intricacies of money management and pioneering the first e-banking platform in Nigeria to digitalize national examination results. Working with Segun Aina, Odunlami Kola-Daisi, Tunji Sobodu, Bayo Odeyale, Kehinde Akinsanya, and Richard Ogunmodede, I found fun sharing a unit with power females Pat Faniran, Kunbi Ademiluyi, Nella Nsa, Seun Omoyele-Dawodu, and Timi Fischer.

I belonged to the generation who had to physically queue up at the JAMB office in Ikoyi to get university entrance examination results. It was either that or wait forever to receive it in the post. It was a thing of great pride to see that problem solved as students and their parents logged in from all across the country. The magnitude of systemic change brought on by our team work led to the broadening of Nigeria's banking industry towards meeting the digital needs of academia. This was Web 1, and we had ample room for growth.

I was lured back to advertising as head of creative and strategic planning at UB40 in Lagos, working on brands like Starcomms Telecom with Sola Lawson and Ireke Amoji, following which I left for Europe, returning to work with British American Tobacco as Brand Manager for the much-loved Rothmans cigarette brand.

BAT (British American Tobacco) was by far the most remarkable female-led team I have worked within. I learned the subtleties of soft power leadership by shadowing Beverly Spencer-Obatoyinbo, who was Head of Trade Marketing and then Marketing Director. She was an articulate strategist, an empathetic, results-oriented manager, and a family woman who somehow infused as much fun into our work as possible. Bev led me to see the combined value in teams and gave me a holistic view of the African business terrain as we compared performance across end markets.

From BAT, I moved to Heineken as Marketing Manager for the new brand Fayrouz. Here, I gained precious insights and experience from working in Europe and the African Middle East region. At Heineken, I gained familiarity with end-to-end production processes and learned the importance of cost optimization with projects of exponential size and scale. With the openness of Chika Osueke, who managed finance for the brand, I also learned to evaluate our profit from raw materials-sourcing to staffing, all the way to production optimization. More importantly, I became adept at process management within a male-dominated working environment. Business leaders like Dele Ajayi, Uche Unigwe, Damian Nwatarali, and Emmanuel Imoaghene made integrating as a female manager in a mostly male workspace easier.

Head hunted to create a corporate marketing team at Samsung West Africa, I gathered relational experience, having never worked with an Asian team before that time. The intriguing reporting structures and merging cultures made a case study for integration in multi-cultural work teams. Working as a curated team of mostly females,

I joined forces with Timi Deinsa-Adamolekun from my STB McCann and Coca-Cola days and with Wendy Adunola Ajuwon from my time at Subaru Motors.

Together, we undertook a tour of the West African markets to meet team members and key distributors of our products in the region. We gained insight that helped revolutionize the Samsung Brand Shop experience across West Africa, creating audio-visual synergies that improved the purchase experience. From our first-hand experience of a desert storm in Mali to the adventure of sharing traditional meals with our key distributor, hosted (and hand-fed) by a sheikh in the desert of Mauritania, we were immersed into the marriage of business with culture across Africa.

In many instances, no senior official had traveled that far inland to meet the often-unseen stakeholders. Our presence assured them of the importance of their contribution to the company's overall success. It also gained the brand immeasurable amounts of goodwill, as well as the respect of women who met us in our official capacity. For me, it was an opportunity to appreciate the vast potential of our region, as well as the pivotal role that women played behind the scenes in most businesses.

On that trip, Absa Gningue impressed me during our time in Senegal and Cote d'Ivoire, explaining the market complexities and the delicate balance necessary to survive and succeed in that part of West Africa. The team then worked to improve corporate brand perception through academic and youth-based CSR (Corporate Social Responsibility) engagements, which we synchronized across end-markets. The greater delight has been to see that many of our signature brand introductions are still in use today.

The rest of my career has been spent learning to improve my understanding of international brands and businesses. I got a taste of non-profit and volunteering work during the earthquake in Haiti, becoming Haitian as I learned to speak the language and travel the land like a local. It became clear that not all market situations have conventional business rules. Haiti was much like Africa, but Haiti was much different from Africa.

I learned Kreyol from a supportive team of young women who took me as their sister and showed me the secrets of their beautiful Caribbean island. Etelka Prosper, Mayena Barbara Chery, Rachel Merisier, Rachel Pratt, and Hugline Jerome gave me network extensions, while Lyndia Dupre gave me street-cred as we walked in places where foreigners did not dare to tread. Our adventures into the interior parts of the island led my group of friends (with Brad Bwasley Lovelace and Taylor Quarles) to build new homes for families displaced by the earthquake. I began to understand the underlying socio-political threads that affect the economy of a nation or region, which made me question the methods of governance and the end-results of corporate business practices.

Through the support of strong mentors, I learned to prioritize personal growth and career development with continuous learning. I have followed that path into new specializations, receiving a Master of Science degree from MIT (Massachusetts Institute of Technology) and going on to a Master of Public Administration from Harvard University's JF Kennedy School of Government (John F. Kennedy School of Government). I have invested years of learning to better understand the business of leadership—especially in Africa. It became the driving force for going into academia so that I might share the lessons garnered from my global apprenticeship with other professionals.

These days, I wear many hats: I am committed to conducting research on culture communication, female entrepreneurship, and frugal tech innovations. I enjoy speaking at conferences where I share what I have learned from my work in marketing, and I offer free or subsidized consulting for MSMEs. I also sit on the board of innovative startups like Bottle Logistics East Africa, Sembe Sierra Leone, House Africa, and UniVirtual. On the other side of the same coin, I teach entrepreneurial marketing and business development to scaling owner-managers at Strathmore University's iBiz Africa Incubator and the E4Impact Accelerator in Kenya. As co-founder and international relations lead at Nampelka GMBH, I contribute directly to the ecosystem by helping female entrepreneurs reach a wider international audience with their products. I also have the honour of being the inaugural Managing Director of ShareHub, a platform that uses games to teach everyday people how to invest in the stock market. I am firmly ensconced at the corner of theory and practice, where real entrepreneurship sits. There is an inexplicable appeal in working at the center of Africa's entrepreneurial oasis and having the opportunity to positively affect growing businesses through business development and leadership training.

Having said the foregoing, Absa and I are proud to add the title of mother to the many roles we serve. With a total of eight children being raised between us, we are women of today's Africa, practicing leadership with wisdom both at home and at work. We note the peculiar challenges of mixing business with family in our environment, and we encourage more women to share the lessons that have helped them to win while straddling multiple lines of leadership.

E. Teach One Another

Our foremost lesson is from the cooperative character of women in general. Nature may have made it easier for the females of our species to nurture, thus equipping us with the first character of leadership. This nurturing, coupled with the ability to retain softer powers, may be the foremost differentiator for women in business. Women possess an intuitive urge to gather and nurture together while actively negotiating the business of life. This book serves as a reminder of the power of our co-learning over time. It comes with tested insight for women within formal organizations and offers guidance to all who seek wisdom for success in business—especially within the African marketplace.

TIPS FROM MOTHER NATURE: Win like a woman!

Understand the difference you make and leverage it positively.

Multitask to maximize your capacity and increase your output.

Learn through successes and failures from other women's journeys.

Believe in teamwork, and invest in yourself and your team.

Raise at least one champion for the cause you are passionate about.

PRACTICE:

List five key interest areas for your personal growth.

CHAPTER 2

Bees: Co-operating for Co-learning

The first time I was "given a title" was while working for Procter & Gamble. It was my first job. I had just turned twenty and considered myself fortunate enough to be recruited from hundreds of applications that week. The process started with thousands of applicants across Africa. I remember hearing the Recruitment Officer, Victor Adebayo, repeating it several times as we complained about how difficult the recruitment test was. I was not expecting to be selected, since I initially knew about the recruitment test from a classmate, Mame Diarra Gueye, who needed my help to prepare for it. She wanted us to be ready for the test. It was a purely coincidental experience of co-learning that led to a fantastic opportunity.

A few weeks passed before I was told I had made it and had been invited for the interviews. What they failed to tell me was that I would have to go through five different interviews! I remember talking so much during those interviews that I came out thirsty and with the resolution that I would not speak a word of English for months. I remember telling myself that we, French speakers, had to work twice as hard as English speakers, trying to speak and understand a language far from our own. But I had to cooperate if I wanted to win that battle.

The interviews were held in a luxury hotel in town on a Friday afternoon. I had almost missed the call of one of the interviewers, as I had disconnected to let my phone charge for a while. I only remember taking a cab *in extremis*, convinced that I just might not pull through to the end. But there I was, waltzing from one table to another, meeting future colleagues like Anass Moutaouakil, who would become my manager, with Ifeoma Okafor and Jean Paul Bom (two colleagues for whom I always had a lot of respect). I considered them more than colleagues. Yes, you can *build honest relationships with your* colleagues. We became real friends over time.

Working for P&G has been an extraordinary experience, my very first journey through human capital development. "Promises made. Promises kept." was the motto of the company, and I was so grateful to work for a company that would claim such a powerful statement and walk the talk. I will never forget those simple sentences written in capital letters at the back of a huge, colorful office in Nigeria. In fact, the company's core values, purpose, principles and vision are focused on the development of its people, and it has been that way for almost two centuries. I would have never imagined that this organization, which I had read about as a case study in marketing classes, would now be employing me. It was quite an eye-opener for me. It was a Sales Representative position, and it appeared that I would spend 90 percent of my time in the field, probably coaching vendors about the same age as my father. But my age has never frightened me: that was quite the opposite!

As the last born in a family of four children (three boys and one girl), I had always been given the opportunity to speak my mind. As an only daughter, it was my duty to take care of the household chores, yet I never felt dominated by the male presence at home.

I've never felt intimidated by men, and the reason might precisely be that I am *Leboue*, an ethnic group that is traditionally matriarchal, where kings took the throne through the mothers' lineage. So, I had no complexes to contend with in front of my brothers or colleagues. I never felt that being a woman was a problem. On the contrary, I associated it with powerful legacies and serious responsibilities.

The flurry of interviews proved fruitful since I was later sent an employment contract for the position of *Key Account Manager*. I had no idea what it meant. For the salary I was to receive, given my age at the time, I was glad for the simple fact that there was the word "manager" in the title. It was during this period that I learned–the hard way–to demystify titles. You will understand my point better as you read through this book.

My job required me to be in Nigeria for a few weeks of training. Again, I had no idea what the training was about, and I did not remember seeing this mentioned anywhere in my contract. I decided to go there with the purpose of understanding my job better. To my surprise, I realized that I was "not a manager" at least not in my theoretical understanding. I was a salesperson! The big title notwithstanding, I was a saleswoman in the markets of Surulere. I became adept at it, rolling in my big van through the crowded streets of Lagos Mainland. I became familiar with busy streets like *Babs Animashaun* and *Adeniran Ogunsanya*. The traffic and the sheer hustle of my new environment were difficult for any newcomer to navigate, but that was the price one had to pay to become a Key Account Manager in Senegal, covering Francophone Africa by learning from the Nigerian end-market.

I remember drafting my letter of resignation several times, and each time, my boss would happen to travel before I submitted it. So I waited. I wanted to feel the pleasure of looking him in the eye when I gave him my resignation letter. Time passed while I waited. We were working at the Procter & Gamble warehouse in Isolo, Lagos. We left the Blue Ribbon Hotel in Ikeja every morning to go to the Isolo warehouse. From there, we loaded the vans with our assistants. We were the VSR (Van Sales Representatives). I say we, because in this adventure, we were three: Jamel Amoakoh Brown, Mathilda Wallace (two colleagues from Ghana), and myself.

Now, let us forget for a moment the pressures of daily sales review meetings in a room containing more than thirty salesmen. Assistants did not participate in the morning reviews. They checked the shipments and washed the cars. Representatives were left to deal with the pressure. Let us remember that I am French-speaking, working in an English-speaking environment and within a vastly different culture. Culturally and socially, the gap was huge. It was the very first time I had ever traveled, and faced several challenges while living far away from my family in a rather fast-paced capital. Those who know Lagos will attest to this.

I remember my mother calling one evening and hearing explosive noises in the background. She asked what it was, and I answered, "fireworks." I was taking the call from under my bed because the sound of gunfire was coming from just outside my hotel room window. A robbery was going on nearby, and residents were taking cover until the trouble passed. I had no option except to be brave. One of my earliest lessons in leadership was knowing how to give situational information without causing the listener to panic. In retrospect, I think this is what forged me as a leader. It was a challenging period, and it made me tough.

Let me tell you the truth: Nigeria gave birth to the woman leader, manager, and entrepreneur I became. I went from being the innocent graduate of the prestigious HECI University to being a fluent Pidgin speaker, counting bundles of money in minutes, like the great *mallams* or wholesalers of Nigeria. In reality, the initial feelings of anger, sadness, and homesickness turned into something different. I had fallen in love with Nigeria—unconditionally. There was the Jollof Rice (which I strongly defended as a Wolof dish from Senegal), and there were other dishes I did not dare try for fear of the hot spice. For months, I contented myself with regular orders of quarter-roasted chicken or pasta with tomato sauce and beef balls.

I got accustomed to the smell of petrol in the air. I got used to the aggressiveness of motorists, the assumed supremacy of pedestrians, the daring stunts of *okada* riders (commercial motorcyclists with pillion riders), and the meandering menace of yellow *Kéké Marwa* (auto tricycles). I even got comfortable with the street vendors shouting "*Piowatta!*" at the top of their lungs. I would later realize that they were actually selling 'Pure Water' in sachets of cold drinking water that quickly quenched one's thirst in the unbearable heat.

Back in Senegal, the learning continued. I had to learn the old sales methods miles away from my home town and far from the familiarity of those who knew me. I had to recruit a team of salespeople for the Distributor as I climbed the corporate ladder by trying to put myself in the shoes of those to whom I gave orders. Using what I had learned in Lagos, I applied it to the local context and developed the local P&G sales force into a formidable one. I was the first sales team member to be recruited and had to prove myself. From a staff strength of eleven people, the distributor had increased to more than sixty salespeople I helped recruit and train. We worked with trucks painted like the ones I had in Nigeria, boasting all the benefits of our products.

To achieve our sales objectives, I was strategic with field visits. I knew every corner of the country. I traveled widely across the regions, and I learned to delegate. I was at the head of a team about the age of my uncles, on average. In fact, one of my direct reports was a classmate's uncle. More than being a woman, I believe that being young was also a managerial handicap, as many of the people around me had difficulties confiding in me. I grew to delegate and understand their reservations.

Yes, to be called the Boss, I had to go to the other side of the table and put myself in the shoes of my salesmen. In most industries, leadership is a club of close-knit associates working with alliances that benefit each side. As women, there is pressure to work across the divides of gender and social structure and earn a place at the leadership table.

A. Learn from Nature

I have always been fascinated by the way Nature works. I find that when it comes to collective success, Nature has a lot to teach us, and bees are a great example of this wisdom. Their organization is much more collaborative and horizontal than it looks, the role of the queen being—apart from reproduction—to foster cohesion and belonging within the hive. Thanks to her pheromones, the queen bee fosters social cohesion as a pillar of survival for her community. If we could take good examples from Mother Nature, then we women would be strategically (and successfully) buzzing like bees!

Males are an essential part of the ecosystem, although their role is limited to reproduction within the bee hive. In human communities, the males often serve as protectors and territorial defense experts, with valuable input while at work. The lesson here is to recognize that if we were able to foster co-operation and belonging through our home networks, we would all be at unimaginable heights–professionally and personally.

Certain lessons specific to the collaborative organization of a beehive can be applied in the professional environment. In subsequent chapters, we compare this analogy with key learnings from the organization of an anthill and examine both as applicable to human society. They are the result of hours spent investigating the behavior of these fascinating species. Although known to be dangerous when they sting, bees are extremely useful to other species that depend on them within the ecosystem. Imagine the crisis of flowering plants without bees for pollination. To the leadership scholar or the corporate observer, certain points catch the eye when studying the organization of bees. These are points we urge each leader to learn from and emulate.

B. Sharing Is Caring

In reality, it would seem that there are six key functions within a hive: nurses, ventilators, keepers, cleaners, foragers, and architects. Contrary to what we imagine, bees are not limited to one role in the organization since, during their life, each bee will move from one function to another. Their organization is truly a learning opportunity: teams talk to each other, and juniors exchange views with seniors. This reminds us of the importance of intergenerational exchanges in our own lives and experiences. As the youngest in most organizations I joined, I know that having the advice of a mentor helped enormously in my career, as well as in my personal life.

I take every opportunity to recognize the people who inspired me throughout my career, many of whom I knew during my time at Procter & Gamble. It is to Kevin Hawkins that I owe the famous "Execute with Excellence" tagline that can be found on my LinkedIn profile. I also learned a lot from Neil Comerford and Standa Vecera, his manager. When I received a birthday card from these two leaders, I thought to myself, "Since my time in Nigeria, they still think of me." This is because they care. Caring really means sharing knowledge, resources, and ideals. This trait is one of the best things we are good at as women.

We only need to translate it into the workplace for a more harmonious experience.

A perfect example of women collaborating in the professional sector remains the "Nana Benz" group. In the 1970s and 1980s, these Togolese businesswomen controlled a large part of West Africa's textile commerce. Powerful and well-versed in business and politics, they drove Mercedes Benz cars as a reflection of their wealth—hence, the group's nickname. But beyond the glamour of their lifestyles, these women were stalwarts who contributed significantly to the regional economy. It was, first and foremost, a collective adventure that characterized the economic mutations of an entire continent, from the early days of the colonial age to the arrival in force of the Chinese in more recent times.

C. Teamwork Means Cooperation, Not Competition

But what is the secret of the Nana Benz group of women? These twenty or so women quickly secured a quasi-monopoly on the trade of Dutch fabrics called Wax Print or *Chigan-vo* (big-money-cloth), as the fabrics were known locally. They simply showed a remarkable solidarity among themselves, making the arrival of new competitors almost impossible.

Coming back to our bee-hive analogy, within the hives, information is vital. When bees exchange information, it is to move things forward without posturing or competing with one another. This is probably what most distinguished the Nana Benz group of business women in Togo. This is the African *ubuntu* spirit, which has helped many organizations develop through relationship marketing. Imagine a marketplace where women would help each other and buy each other's products! This is one of the particular reasons why my NGO, JEADER, has recently signed a partnership with a consortium of women. With more than 79,108 women across Senegal, leading across different value chains, if these women were to agree to pay 1000 Fcfa ($2) per week each, they would have raised 3.797.184.000 Fcfa ($6,781,720) within twelve months. Just imagine for a second their impact in terms of financial sovereignty and the endless possibilities of rolling this out across the continent.

D. Embrace Diversity and Good Leadership

We are all different, but what unites us is much stronger than what divides us. In order to increase the strength of the hive, the queen is fertilized by a dozen bees from other hives. Here, the diversity of input by way of skills, opinions, and attitudes counts. One must accept the plurality of points of view to create optimal value. The queen bee's role is extremely important since she is selected and fed to her peak by all the bees in the hive.

I have been living in Abidjan since 2018, and am impressed by women's perceived place in different households. This can be explained by the history of Queen Abla Pokou, who had no choice but to flee from the current Ghana to settle with the Baule people on the territory that became Côte d'Ivoire. This queen was followed by her servants, her faithful soldiers, and all those people who recognized themselves in her by crossing the Comoe river into a new land.

Leadership is the natural ability to engender trust that leads to being followed. Simply agreeing to stand behind a person seems utopian nowadays. However, nothing prevents us from bringing our solidarity to women leaders who already have privileged positions in their respective industries. Our communities thrive when women support one another and foster growth through mutual support. The success of one female is valuable social currency because it encourages other females to try, succeed, and establish a pattern of progress that becomes positively infectious to society.

E. Bee Useful to the Ecosystem

Bees primarily produce honey, but they have an even more important environmental mission as pollinators. Bees work the magic that allows plants to reproduce as Mother Nature intended. The role of bees is to forage for flowers and bring pollen back to the hive to make nectar, honey, and wax. They participate in nearly 80 percent of the pollination of plant species. They are, therefore, the indispensable link in the survival, evolution, and organic reproduction of plants.

In truth, beyond the social organization they have built, they are useful to their ecosystem and community. This usefulness means that other species will be protective of bees to keep the balance of nature. It is the same within work teams, where systemic usefulness is a form of self-preservation. Let us, therefore, be useful to the ecosystem where we operate!

TIPS FROM MOTHER NATURE: Buzz like a bee!

Remember to communicate and share relevant information.

Remember to stay as "sweet as honey" with your words.

Remember that each one contributes to the whole ecosystem.

Remember to feed your teammates when needed.

Remember that cooperation is better than competition.

PRACTICE:

Identify five ways to serve your business ecosystem.

CHAPTER 3

Ants: Focus on Strategic Strengths

The organizational wisdom seen in bees is also true for ants. Did you know, for example, that ants are actually the most aggressive living beings in terms of strategy? Ants wage territorial wars, even if it means exterminating other species to recover as much food as possible for the ant community. They use ingenious military strategies by analyzing their enemies and attacking as a group with the force and cohesion of military troops.

The anthill is an excellent example of efficient creativity, where the business of living is taken care of, and the operational side of ant life is managed without the prying eyes of predators and other species. Communication is seamless as hundreds and thousands of ants march in unison towards whatever target the group has set for them. As women in leadership, our internal and external communication strategies need to be as seamless as the marching of ants.

A. Find Your Voice

Finding one's leadership voice means using the natural endowment of skills and characters blended with the requirements of culture to express ourselves in business. Our communication goals may be varied, but our intentions are often aligned as we all seek to connect our businesses with the buying public. Setting clear communication goals can be tricky when speaking to more than one demographic. As a rule, women leaders tend to fare better when they can find the right words and ways to translate critical business decisions to the team and then empower the team to likewise carry those decisions in messages to the public.

Growing up in Surulere was an experience full of business lessons for me. Whereas Absa came to know Surulere as an adult, I had grown up in that busy, bustling neighbourhood, and its business was in my blood. It was a commercial center and a residential haven growing fast and adding to the intriguing character of the island city called Lagos. The Lagos palate had a reputation for its love of seafood, and our neighbourhood had a favorite fishmonger. She hawked her merchandise along the streets, carrying the fish in a deep plastic bucket packed with ice chips to preserve the freshness. She carried the big bucket on her head, balanced expertly as she walked with a slightly exaggerated swagger. She was gifted with a clear, sonorous voice, as strong and pleasing as silk threads and with similar smoothness and elegance. She would call out in her teasing, familiar voice, and the second part of the call was delivered in a slightly husky tone.

"Gbeetuoo! Omi akerese!"

It was loud enough that one could hear her three streets over, yet soft enough to elicit smiles from the women who ran outside to patronize her. As a child, I never understood the meaning of her words, but I always listened out for her. I often ran out to call her on those days when my grandmother wanted to cook fish for dinner. The magic was in the tone of the hawker's call. Although I was young, I, too, was caught up in the magic of the fishmonger's tone. When I grew into womanhood, I finally understood the message in its entirety. To the adult demographic, that message had been clear all along: the fish hawker was calling housewives to buy fresh fish, impress their husbands at dinner, and be rewarded with "sweet water." The best part of the hawker's advertising message was cloaked in cultural innuendo. Yet, it encouraged each woman to buy fresh fish from her.

Fish on the island was affordable, regardless of the differences in family budget. She had small fish, medium-sized fish, big fish, and even extra-large types that only the wealthy could afford to buy. Yet she appealed to diverse pocket depths in the same words and with the same meaning. She found the one thing that housewives had in common and addressed that sentiment in her communication. It had taken decades, but I finally learned the secret of the fishmonger's advertising strategy. By thinking like an ant, the fishmonger was appealing to the group by addressing the individual.

The point of this passage is not to debate the nature of the ant's thought processes. We seek to draw attention to the meticulously crafted social strategy adopted by these little creatures, believing that if we, as humans, are able to integrate these inclusive mechanisms into our leadership strategy, we will develop better in an increasingly asocial society.

B. No Negative Complexes

The ant plays a vital role in the conservation of the natural environment and represents a model of organization and communication. Despite its relatively small size, it can be formidable to the enemy. We can learn a lot from the strategic efficiency of ant communities and the methods with which they achieve collective purpose through subtle communication. No one ant is more important than the other; each one contributes uniquely to the community. From the speed with which sugar-loving ants attack a sweet dish and cart away its contents, it is clear that our individual sizes or team structures do not limit us; our mindsets and visions do.

C. You Are Not "Too Small"

Have you ever noticed that an ant can carry things on its head? Ants have the uncanny ability to dismantle the target and cart it away as little bits that are expertly transported to the food store. These little beasts are not afraid of anything. They know they can count on others when they need manual labor or collective stinging strength to attack in times of trouble.

Although its appearance does not suggest strength, the ant can carry up to four times its own weight, trekking over almost a kilometer. But more than the weight we each carry at different levels of responsibility, an ant will only carry a burden it knows to share with its sister-ants. In most cases, this weight will be divided and delegated so that each ant is part of the whole commitment.

Therefore, let us know how to measure the weight of the burdens we commit ourselves to carry, because our team members will also be part of that commitment.

D. Stay Alert, Keep Busy

In many religions, the ant is cited for its wisdom and its level of energy and activity. Of all the insects mentioned in the Holy Qur'an, the ant holds a special place. The Prophet Sulaiman, known for his wisdom, speaks of his encounter with the small creatures. Similarly, the Holy Bible mentions the ant in the book of Proverbs, credited to King Solomon advising mankind to "Go to the ant, O sluggard, observe her ways and be wise." It is not common to see an idle ant. Ants are usually busy, usually in motion, occupied by their purpose. In Buddhism, ants are seen as sentient beings, and insects, bugs, or worms are not to be trampled upon as they go about their daily business because these insects also play an important role in creation.

In a society that places much weight on the dictates of religion and tradition, women in business can learn from the ant as a symbol of entrepreneurship, creativity, discipline, diligence, and commitment to the environment. The ant does its business despite the kind of terrain it finds itself in. Its sense of organization, the social life of its community, the efficacy of communication, the collectivity of industry, the understanding of frugality and economy, the propensity for hard work, and the visible social cohesion combine to make the ant an exceptional example cited throughout the ages.

Looking around us, we all know how to identify an ant-woman. She is an active, industrious person, ready to undertake the tasks that provide for her family. She is an excellent time manager with no tolerance for slander or gossip noises along the way. This does not mean that the ant-like woman should be anti-social. When observed, we can see some ants pause to offer a brief greeting along the lines of work, but each one continues quickly on her way to completing the task at hand. In this way, women also need discernment to socialize without compromising the mission.

E. No Fellow Left Behind

The solidarity of the ants is a lesson worth learning for efficient, co-dependent teams that work towards a common goal. Did you know that ants are able to ingest food and regurgitate it when needed? When a sister-ant is in need, a meal of regurgitated food sustains the needy one so that the collective work can go on. In reality, ants have two stomachs. One is used to store food for their consumption, while the second is used to store food to share with other ants. This can be seen as Mother Nature's own strategy for mutual support in a co-dependent community.

The acceptance letter for my Harvard degree arrived within weeks of the confirmation that we were expecting twin babies. As my husband and I discussed the pros and cons of returning to school with a high-risk pregnancy, I realized that life (like Nature) does not pause for milestone events. I had to balance my home life raising a 9-year-old son with my commitment to managing the MIT Africa conference and investment forum that year and resuming studies at HKS (Harvard Kennedy School). I found unexpected support in my father, who traveled from Nigeria to look after us during that time. In traditional Igbo culture, *omugwo*–the preparation for the arrival of a baby–is considered very important. The grandmother-to-be spends considerable time, effort, and money caring for the expectant mother and her household. Typically, the women traveled for *omugwo* and not the men. But times were different, and I am blessed with a father who has vast experience with babies and is openminded enough to take on such a maternal role. This gave me the freedom to take on a full class schedule.

During lunch breaks, I would remain in class, unable to navigate the stairs from the Forum and too tired to drag my big bump onto the lunchtime queue. To my surprise, classmates would return from lunch with tokens left on my table–a banana, an orange, a protein bar, a milkshake, or any other healthy snack to keep me fueled. Sometimes, I met the love offerings on my table when I was not even there. Like my father, the men of my class were heroically supportive.

I went into labor during our quant finals. Still, I managed to finish the exam before driving myself over to Beth Israel for the delivery. I took a selfie before the delivery to assure my study group that I was okay. My husband maintains that my African-woman pride would not allow me to call an ambulance and break the serene peace of the Kennedy School yard. I was determined to balance motherhood with learning without disturbing the other, and my community provided me with the means to do so.

Amazingly, my classmates took turns preparing bulk meals and filled my freezer with delicious culturally-diverse food that lasted through the difficult early months. Sister-queens like Fadumo Dayib, Deborah Bailey, Vedette Gavin, and Phyllis Johnson would come over to my house and help out while we took some much-needed time off from our hectic school schedules. As I juggled academic work with the business of raising three small children, I was embraced by my class community, who fed me out of their second stomachs, just like Mother Nature's ants.

This process is known as *trophallaxis* and allows a colony of ants to work efficiently. This way, the ants looking for food can store some for those that stay behind to protect the queen and the nest. Imagine a network where women would be willing to contribute to the whole effort on behalf of their sisters. This theory of shared responsibility is the very basis of *tontines*, rotational *chamas*, *esusu* savings groups, and participatory financing!

In 2006, researchers at the University of Bristol, in England, spent countless hours analyzing ants in search of food. They found that the two leader ants and the followers appeared to be working as a pair. A leader ant, for example, could run and reach food four times faster if alone, yet it works with a follower ant to teach it how to find food and remember its location. The teaching ant seems to adapt its pace to the ability of the learning ant.

Since ant colonies seem to function with seamless communication, researchers are analyzing what we should be imitating based on their example. Women in business could adopt the same spirit and take the time to share and care about our sisters while helping fellow female entrepreneurs or business leaders gain knowledge and transferable skills. The role of each one is essential to the success of the whole enterprise, as the ant shows us.

TIPS FROM MOTHER NATURE: Think like an ant!

Remember to understand your place in the structure.

Remember to stay connected to group strengths: You are not "too small"!

Remember that each one carries a share of the whole.

Remember that each one is responsible of sharing their knowledge to another.

Remember to use that second stomach!

PRACTICE:
Pinpoint five of your team's key "shareable" strengths.

CHAPTER 4

Cats: Grooming Is Perception Management

The cat is a well-groomed creature, preoccupied with ridding itself of unpleasantness while preserving an immaculate exterior. In business, we need to present with the cleanliness of cats and the elegance of brides. To the average African, a bride is a family's pride and joy, a reason for joining communities to celebrate. The decorations on the bride are a testament to the successful raising of a member of one community, of scaling into adulthood, and of the beginning of a new unit in another community. A bride is a symbol of united bloodlines and consolidated assets, shown in the beauty of her attire and the quality of her appearance. According to the Yoruba proverb, "Henna on the bride's feet is like a clue for the groom to read."

It is not difficult to identify an African bride in the midst of a dancing crowd. When applied to business, the same principle applies to perception management. A clean image with visible integrity in the habits of the leader and the company are valuable traits in business. How we present ourselves and our businesses affects how we are perceived by our teammates and evaluated by those looking in from the outside.

Perception matters more than most leaders think; often, a win rides on the back of positive perceptions. More than 2 years after leaving P&G, I was contacted by a headhunter via LinkedIn. I initially thought it was a scam until I realized I was talking to the HR manager of Samsung Electronics from the headquarters. After an interview with the general manager of the Senegal office, I would later learn that I got the job. Now, as much as P&G allowed me to give value to the human factor, Samsung allowed me to appreciate the value of our work as individuals and as a team.

We worked morning and night, weekdays and weekends when necessary. In my opinion, we worked maybe a little too much. The language barrier was also to be considered as we had to embrace a new culture and manage perception. Initially, I could not tell if my boss was happy or furious. I could not tell from his facial expression, perhaps because his culture prioritized emotional control. He once claimed that I had three brains because I was so curious. It was important that I was curious and willing to learn new things. I had a brand to represent as Samsung West Africa's Marketing & Communications Coordinator. I perceived a need for better cultural interaction and quickly started to learn and understand Korean. This effort gave me an advantage and made working within that culture easier.

As people look at you, they should also see what your brand represents. With successful businesses, the first brand ambassador is usually the business owner. The culture of visual evaluation is common to African communities, and onlookers take cues from how the business or person is portrayed. From the first words that come forth when introduced to the palpable sense of accomplishment that follows a good meeting or business encounter, the brand and business should be well represented in every situation.

We have modeled this chapter after the metaphysical African cat: comfortable indoors or outdoors and able to mix the business of rodent hunting with the pleasure of a shared hearth. As women in business, we are like the proverbial cat with nine lives, surviving one emergency after the other and living to tell stories of our victories. We have found it helpful to teach entrepreneurs how to develop a deliberate brand persona to guide the business and communicate purpose to the public.

A. Look the Part

It is crucial to have a no-mess strategy for business. With physical and financial hygiene, women in business can keep pestilence at bay. Well-kept records, ethical business dealings, accountability and auditability, and other good practices go a long way to strengthening the public image and reassuring all stakeholders. The stories of failed African businesses and scandal-tossed entrepreneurial giants are known to many. Yet, the testimony of honest women doing business across Africa goes largely unheard.

As women in business, we owe ourselves a duty to promote one another and increase the incidences of good reports about African businesses that women are leading. Cats have very visible personalities. In the same way, leadership should be visible. It is important to look like the leader you are growing to be. A cat spends considerable amounts of time grooming itself privately. As women in business, we must prioritize grooming for career development as the route to self-actualization. Like the all-surviving cat, a cool, clean demeanour is built on hours of personal preparation. Look like the expert that you are, and let your knowledge confirm your look.

As an ambassador for your business, showcase the creativity (like bridal henna) that differentiates your brand and celebrates your accomplishments.

B. Be the Story

Cats establish physical contact early in the interaction process as a way of introduction. This introduction sets the pace for future interactions. As a Nigerian-born extrovert, introductions are typically easy for me, as I am able to walk up to just about anyone and strike up an engaging conversation. I have also had the privilege of working with outspoken females like Absa, who are exceptional communicators. Yet, it is clear that not everyone can navigate interactions with such ease. Teaching entrepreneurship at E4Impact Kenya has given me much insight into the interaction challenges that many African entrepreneurs face on a day-to-day basis. In one of my favourite class exercises, I ask each student to introduce themselves and their businesses in three simple sentences. This is how I lead them to elevator pitching.

With practice, the class soon learns that introductions are easier when both parties can relate to the entrepreneurial story. The outstanding performers learn to craft the story of how they got on the path, showing where they are and where they would like to be. For others, the idea of speaking to an audience of strangers is quite daunting, and eloquent self-introductions come with even more practice.

In African communities, many are still in the process of getting comfortable talking business with women. Many times, women have had to lead without loud attention and make progress without any visible aggression. Women in leadership have had to craft our mission messages carefully, bearing in mind the respectful, humble demeanour many tribal structures prescribe. With that backdrop, we find that some women are culturally (or traditionally) unable to make the usual pitch introductions. For these cases, we advise that a loosely-formed introduction should be crafted from three essential pitch questions:

Who are you? What do you do differently? How does it benefit the listener?

By answering these simple questions, anyone can make up an elevator pitch and generate interest as a next step. These ready-made introductions can be plugged in early in the conversation, as early as just after the initial "hello," and can be adjusted to suit each scenario. Not everyone is comfortable being an extrovert, but everyone can learn how to start an interesting business conversation. When we own our stories, we show the world that in telling these stories, we confirm our journeys as examples of business victories in this terrain. In every class, I encourage entrepreneurs to practice endless grooming, present a cool front, and tell the story because the world is listening.

C. Understand Sounds and Symptoms

Did you know that the cat always lands on its feet? As leaders, life gives us several opportunities to do just the same. A few months before leaving Procter & Gamble, I could feel that I did not have much time left with my employer. Indeed, at the time, the company was preparing to review all employees in Senegal, and I had taken the lead, highlighting my skills via LinkedIn. We must understand sounds and symptoms in our working environment. I literally jumped like a cat at the opportunity to showcase my skills, opening a new door while another was about to close. It was an excellent preparatory period for growth planning in my career. I did not know what the future would hold, but I was preparing for it actively. I had no idea that beyond the experience I was going to gain in Marketing & Communications at Samsung, I was also going to meet the person with whom I would write a book—12 years later!

Cats are sensitive to emotions and the characters of persons who come into the same space. In the same vein, we humans know whether or not we *feel* something or someone. It is important to understand the attitudes or reactions to our presentations and adjust accordingly. Female intuition means that we can sense acceptance or displeasure in much the same way as a cat can sense empathy or antagonism. We intuitively read the room. As women in business, we need a fundamental understanding of emotional intelligence. We must be able to react to situations and make corrective decisions with the same cool demeanour that makes the cat unique.

While women are focused on business and career growth in a highly-competitive, male-dominated environment, grooming is often from the top down. Expectedly, after a while, the groomed become strong enough to groom others in turn. This is the reason cats teach kittens how to bat, scratch, catch, and run in a bid to impart skills necessary for the functional aspects of the cat business.

Women make the best deliberate mentors, and the old communal way of life has given the example of African entrepreneurship its distinct flavour. By creating the virtual village to raise the next generation of leaders, we can begin to mentor women of like minds and raise more cool cats for the growing global economy.

D. Defend Whenever Necessary

Pitching and self-introduction can be likened to an open door, where clients of different kinds walk in and pet the friendly cat. On the other hand, leadership must be alert to danger as "contact-auditing" (touching everything carefully) and self-defense are important next steps along the road to scaling. When alerted to danger, the purring cat becomes a formidable enemy, baring fangs and growling from the same pleasantly rubbed belly. The cat is always ready to defend its territory from suspected assailants. This psychological ownership translates to business leadership, making it necessary to apply caution in unfamiliar avenues of business.

The cat strategy is built on a feline instinct for self-preservation and selfless protection of one's territory. This finds expression in business, as each woman in leadership learns to institute anti-pilfering plans for concepts and business ideas while preventing wastage and operational indiscipline. Like a mouse patrol, set to catch potential offenders before harm is inflicted on the business, the cat-like leader is ever vigilant and always nimble.

E. Interact at Every Opportunity

The cat is sensitive to personal interaction, and interaction is key to growth. With a well-worded message, a well-timed introduction, a well-planned event, or a well-orchestrated meeting, interaction can be encouraged and then leveraged for growth. Interaction is not intuitive to all, which means that some of us need to learn how to be more open to social sharing. When dealing with customers, the basis of interaction is our work in relation to the service provided to each customer. By having clarity on internal roles and external needs, shy people can communicate their thoughts and gradually improve through interaction.

Cats give good feedback. With a purr, the cat communicates satisfaction, and with a snarl, it communicates displeasure. Clients and teammates are much the same when personal reactions are considered. Conciliatory interaction helps leaders have a listening and learning attitude when it comes to problem-solving. By learning the ways of the cat, women leaders can commit to the nimble practice of interactive messaging, territorial defense, and continuous grooming.

TIPS FROM MOTHER NATURE: Groom like a cat!

Remember to have a no-mess strategy for business.

Remember to practice pitching and self-introduction.

Remember to keep grooming talents for business.

Remember to protect your assets from "rodents" and pests.

Remember to interact positively with each customer.

PRACTICE:

List five positive perception objectives that customers should have about your business.

CHAPTER 5

Monkeys: Flexibility from Group Security

We attended a meeting of The Potato Council in Nairobi, Kenya. The agricultural entrepreneurs and agribusiness stakeholders had gathered at the KEPHIS (Kenya Plant Health Inspectorate Service) campus in Karen, just at the edge of the great Ngong Forest. We sat through several presentations, trying our best not to be distracted by the group of monkeys swinging playfully through the trees and venturing near enough to peer through the windows of the hall. It was mid-morning, and the tea service had arrived a little earlier than the time shown on the agenda. The speaker rounded up quickly and informed us that it was time for our tea break and an opportunity to stretch our legs. Some participants took their cups and wandered towards the open grounds beyond our meeting hall.

A. Expect Monkey Business

Hearing sudden shouts and loud laughter from inside, we hurried outside to see what happened. One daring young monkey had ambled up to a member of our group and taken away their paper plate with samosas, spring rolls, and *mandazis* on it. The monkey then casually climbed into a low-hanging branch, flanked by a group of menacing, older monkeys. As we watched the paper plate float back down from the monkey's perch, the hostess told us that it was common for monkeys to attend meetings on that campus. They knew intuitively that human gatherings came with food, and they waited and watched for those humans who were not aware of how daring monkeys could get.

The monkeys at KEPHIS somehow knew that humans attending these meetings were more likely to be non-combative and would likely see the funny side of sharing a snack with primate cousins.

There was no chance to negotiate. The monkeys had won without bargaining or needing to fight for the food. More than anything else, the younger monkey's daring feat was emboldened by the presence of older, more experienced monkeys, who would defend the younger one should the need arise. There was a strategic reason why the monkeys chose to inhabit trees closer to the meeting hall.

Women are known to work with similar long-term outcomes in mind. This means using intuition with psychological negotiations and mostly choosing our battles wisely. Leading as women in African business means learning the industry's behavior and knowing how to negotiate the conflicting situations we face daily.

B. Respect Cultural Obstacles

Working in Kenya has meant experiencing different cultures within the same ecosystem and learning from each one. The Maasai tribe was one of those with whom I lived in a rural setting and from whom my family learned a lot about Nature and the care of our natural environment. The colorful Maasai attire is one of Kenya's most symbolic cultural icons, with a way of life that embraces the old nomadic traditions while incorporating modern technology. In Maasai custom, the cow belongs to the man as head of the household, while the milk belongs to the woman as the one in charge of family nutrition. Maasai tradition permits women to do business with milk but not with cows. In a feat of modern ingenuity, the women of Odupa Women's Cooperative Society in Narok, Kenya, have come together as a *chama* group to collectively supply milk to bulk buyers and use the excess milk to produce yoghurt.

Even more remarkable is the women's choice of brand spokesperson in Daniel Kipilosh. Since most business is done by men traditionally, the Odupa women chose a man to serve as brand ambassador and spokesman at business meetings. The *chama* receives contributions and payments for the milk supplied, while the women use the increased income to finance innovative production technology, like solar-powered, donkey-mountable, refrigerated mobile milk tanks from MaziwaPlus, which help to preserve fresh milk over longer distances. They also use their collective funds to support one another by re-investing in complementary businesses. The profits also help to pay for their children's education.

The production of yoghurt creates employment for several members of the Narok community, and the product brings income to the local economy. Without ruffling traditional feathers or creating financial friction in the home, these Maasai women keep their money out of sight in digital wallets on their mobile phones, while the group funds are managed by a *chama* manager who is one of the women leaders in the community. Due to the respectful way in which the women approached the Narok elders, they were able to do business with goodwill from the community while enjoying the support of leadership in accordance with culture.

C. Recruit Like Minds as Stakeholders

For the same strategic reasons, women in business need peer advocacy and group security within their chosen industry. When formally registered businesses are backed by advocacy groups and relevant peers, the ecosystem usually gives way by making room for the businesses covered within those advocacy groups. It is also easier and more beneficial to negotiate as a group and enjoy the benefits as individual businesses. Like the monkeys differentiating between non-combative humans and the more predatory kind, women in leadership must frequently distinguish cultural negotiators from strictly professional bargainers.

In most indigenous communities, the act of bargaining or commercial negotiation is learned early in life. Visits to the local market reveal the eternal dance between buyer and seller, where the tune is dictated by the negotiating ability of the stronger party. As adults in business, we see the same patterns repeated in our business negotiations, with the additional demand for subtlety and mutual respect as bargains are struck. For many female-led businesses, we recommend that negotiations be done with one or more team members for support. It is paramount to understand the negotiator's background and the context within which they are meeting your team. It also helps to have people on your side who share common values with the negotiator and who, therefore, understand the micro-psychology behind decisions made on either side.

D. Practice Conflict-Free Negotiation

The earliest experiences in our lives come with some conflict in tow. From the moment most babies are pushed (or pulled) out of the womb, they realize they are not ready to leave the warm comfort of that haven to face the harsh realities of our world. This is the first instance of desires conflicting with reality. Most babies soon find out how to make the best of this human experience. As leaders in our business or personal roles, we are constantly navigating social conflicts to the best of our ability. We learn how to influence our environment by gaining knowledge and improving interpersonal skills.

In most cases, we first meet interpersonal conflict within the four walls of our own homes. Siblings usually provide enough instances of conflict buildup and peaceful resolutions. We often learn our first lessons in conflict resolution from our parents and older members of our communities who can help us deal with this. The benefit of past experiences will add a culturally appropriate perspective to the eventual solution.

From nuclear family conflicts with resource sharing, conflicts with usage and ownership, conflicts with chores or responsibilities, or conflicts with no reasonable reasons at all, most young Africans get a good chance to prepare for the bigger, graver conflicts that await us in the outer world. Depending mainly on each one's temperament, upbringing, and exposure to conflict resolution, we go into the world with preconceptions regarding conflicts and how we are meant to manage them. These resolution experiences replicate themselves in our businesses, too.

As modern social structures give increasing opportunities to women, conflict-free business negotiations will allow more female leaders to surmount gender bias. Interventions can only be fruitful after conflicting parties have acknowledged the issues involved, reviewed the factors at stake, and realized that an amicable resolution is needed. As with countries, the same basic principle applies to people. By selecting strategies supporting intervention instead of confrontation, we can promote reconciliation within our teams and encourage better conflict resolution.

E. See Leadership Beyond Conflict

In some cultures, a small conflict may be allowed to "outgrow" itself. The people involved are often asked to walk away and allow things to settle. This can be helpful. It gives each party the time and distance to view things from a different perspective. And yes, we have finally arrived at the meat of this matter. Conflicts are about *issues*. They are not about people, but they are about the issues that affect those people. Issues make people act and react in certain ways, which in turn may bring more actions and reactions into play.

When we look at conflicts from that perspective, we can better analyze the issues involved and separate those from our feelings about the people involved. As the lunchtime crowd returned from our Potato Council meeting, we noticed a plastic plate full of deliberately leftover snacks near the copse of trees. Beyond conflict, the reparative role of leadership is to find a balance in the system where both the monkeys and the meeting attendees can enjoy a shared positive experience.

TIPS FROM MOTHER NATURE: Be agile like a monkey!

Remember to see the funny side of every situation.

Be agile, but remember to stay close to the source of business.

Remember to identify non-combative stakeholders and low-hanging fruits.

Remember to negotiate with cultural understanding.

Remember that advocacy works better with group security.

PRACTICE:
Join a business interest group or start one with five partners.

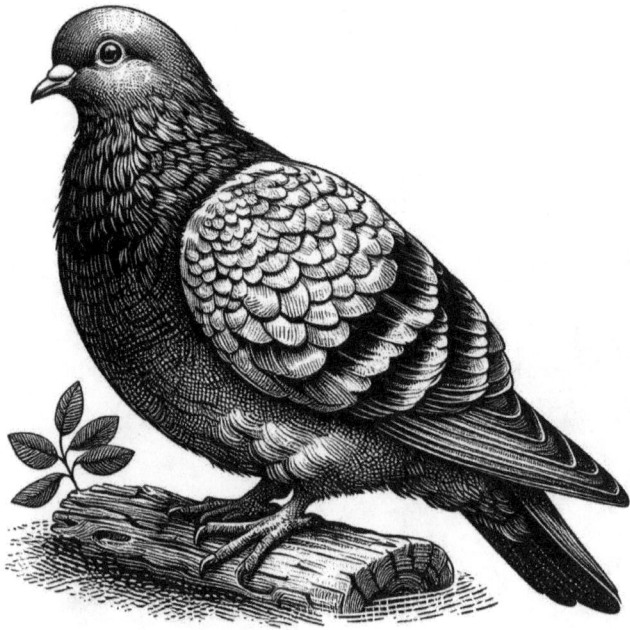

CHAPTER 6

Pigeons: Serial Multitaskers: Masters of Many Trades

I have always been fascinated by pigeons. Beyond the stunning array of their feathers, I have always seen in these birds a unique form of freedom intertwined with a profound sense of loyalty–two values that are very dear to my heart. When I was young, my older brother Youssou raised pigeons, which caused him endless trouble. At one point, he preferred spending time with his flock of pigeons over studying his lessons. My parents tried everything to dissuade him, but nothing worked; he harbored an unmatched love for these birds that would scatter throughout the neighborhood but always return.

I remember one time my father beat him severely because he failed his exams due to his obsession with the pigeons. On another occasion, he confronted some neighborhood boys who claimed ownership of various pigeons. Since he initially couldn't identify them, these conflicts became more frequent until he found rings with initials for the birds. My brother always managed to recognize his pigeons, insisting, "Each pigeon is unique with its specific characteristics and personality."

A. Find Your Way Back

What truly fascinates me is the pigeon's ability to find its way back home, as I had a hard time navigating without the GPS. As women professionals, we often find ourselves lost amidst personal and professional responsibilities. Even our physical selves can seem out of our control, bombarded by ads urging us to use various products to look clearer or slimmer.

How do we return to our roots? How do we get back to where we truly belong?

An African proverb says, "When you don't know where you're going, go back to where you came from."

For centuries, homing pigeons have been messengers for humans. In times of war, they could find their way back to their nests despite distance and harsh conditions. This ability was considered a reliable communication method until the end of World War I. What is this inner compass that allows such a seemingly fragile creature to remember all this information? It's the perception of the Earth's magnetic field. Pigeons have iron oxide particles at the base of their skull and neck muscles, which act like a compass, moving in response to the magnetic field and stimulating certain brain nerves.

An October 2023 study by researchers from Ohio State University and the University of Iowa revealed that in a test where pigeons had to categorize different elements by pecking a button on the left or right, their performance improved from 55 percent to 95 percent correct responses through trial and error. Scientists then conducted the same experiments with artificial intelligence and observed a similar learning process with AI, also reducing errors gradually as it learns.

Now, going back to the professional perspective, returning to the starting point can be both stressful and, depending on the situation, an admission of failure. Between 2011 and 2012, when I decided to resign from Samsung Electronics to start my own business, I felt like I was going backward. This return to the starting point was motivated by an old dream and a promise I made to my father before he passed away 10 years earlier. I felt it was the right time to create my clothing brand and hire my mother after her retirement. This childhood dream materialized in 2012 when I felt the urge to venture into entrepreneurship. That's how DESI'GNING and SAMA BOSS were born, a business that eventually led to the founding of JEADER (Young African Entrepreneurs for Economic and Regional Development) in 2014. This organization promotes leadership through entrepreneurship with partners in over 25 African countries and the diaspora.

Today, my brand, ABC-Love Africa. Wear Africa, created back then, has become a 150-square-meter concept store in Dakar-Ouakam, employing five people and exporting to over fifteen countries, including Côte d'Ivoire, France, the USA, Nigeria, South Africa, Ghana, and Madagascar. We also have two 150-square-meter Airbnb locations, a photo studio, a boutique, and a discussion room. We offer marketing services (community management, logos, flyers) to small and medium-sized enterprises, as well as personal branding through graphic design services.

B. Learn from Your Mistakes

What if the secret of pigeons was in their ability to learn from their mistakes and remember those lessons to refine their outcomes? As women managers, we often feel as though we do not have the luxury of making mistakes, whether because we must maintain our composure in front of those who may be waiting for us to slip up or because we strive to excel in all roles—chef, mother, homemaker, and manager. We navigate our responsibilities with the understanding that nothing will be handed to us on a silver platter.

At the start of my career at IBM, I never imagined thriving in such a prestigious organization led by a woman with such a captivating smile. I was naturally impressed by Ginni Rometty's stature. Ginni was the epitome of leadership and innovation, always thinking outside the box and emphasizing that how we work and lead is as important as what we achieve. As the ninth Chairman, President, and CEO of IBM, she transformed the 100-year-old company, reinventing 50 percent of its portfolio, building a $25 billion hybrid cloud business, and establishing IBM's leadership in AI and quantum computing.

Ginni often spoke of "Wild Ducks," inspired by IBM founder Thomas J. Watson Sr. and Søren Kierkegaard's story. The term refers to innovators within organizations who are given the freedom to break norms and rules. These "wild ducks" are crucial for driving innovation. This is how I learned at IBM that every mistake is a valuable lesson—they help us move forward and grow. This environment encouraged me to experiment as a marketing manager, leading to many unconventional ideas to help salespeople market the Cloud, which wasn't widely known at the time.

From campaigns like "Batman v Superman: Dawn of Justice" to "Angry Birds," I created initiatives featuring fictional heroes to recognize the best salespeople across our territory, covering over 70 countries in the Middle East, Africa, and Turkey. This creativity earned me recognition from the headquarters in Armonk for bringing "extraordinary" marketing initiatives to life.

Additionally, thanks to IBM's "Dare to Innovate" campaigns, I developed a platform that won the MEA WILD DUCK Award in Abu Dhabi. This platform, powered by AI (Watson), anticipated young people's predispositions, allowing us to identify potential future doctors, engineers, pilots, writers, and more based on their MBTI personality tests.

C. Try as Many Options as You Can

Unlike humans, pigeons do not try to establish rigid rules. Instead, they use trial and error to learn and remember lessons from their mistakes. This approach might seem contrary to the common managerial advice to stay FOCUSED. However, in certain situations, the key might be to test multiple options to determine which works best. As marketers, we often use A/B testing, always having a backup solution based on the market's response.

A prime example of the need for agility was the COVID-19 pandemic, which required quick action, creative solutions, and frugal innovation to avoid being overwhelmed by the crisis. I recall some seemingly wild innovations that thankfully led to systems still in use today in various healthcare settings: the pedal-operated handwashing station, the portable ventilator, and 3D-printed masks, among others.

D. Be Prepared for Multitasking

Did you know that pigeons performed better than humans when multitasking? First, multitasking is a skill, so we need to understand and practice a lot to find the balance between efficiency and productivity. The old saying that practice makes perfect is especially true here. The more those pigeons performed the task, the better they became at doing it faster. Now, pigeons can switch between two tasks as quickly as humans—and quicker than humans in certain situations.

E. Be Alert

Pigeons not only learn from their mistakes but also from their perceptions. They can distinguish between friendly and threatening actions, recognizing individuals who feed them versus those who chase them away. Similarly, leaders learn to identify allies and differentiate them from detractors—not to become overly cautious, but to know how to collaborate and network effectively with supporters. Pigeons often fly alone but come together in groups to share food. Be alert enough to recognize when you need to work alone and when you need more hands to help you win your battles.

TIPS FROM MOTHER NATURE: Be adaptive like a pigeon!

Remember to find your way back when you no longer know where to go.

Remember to learn from your mistakes; they are your most precious lessons.

Remember to try as many options as you can.

Remember not to be scared of multitasking; find the balance!

Remember to be alert! Recognize and fly with your supporters.

PRACTICE:

Identify five ways to learn and reveal your talents while learning from your mistakes.

CHAPTER 7

Owls: Visioning and Intuitive Clarity

It was a Monday morning breakfast meeting in Nairobi's high-brow banking district, and Equity Bank CEO Mr. James Mwangi was introducing his team to the gathering of stakeholders, VIPs, and high-net-income customers. I noticed that when he introduced the company secretary, Mary Wangari Wamae, he complimented her for working with intuition and emphasized that the bank had gained much mileage by simply listening to the hunches from her female leadership.

I was not surprised to hear that. As applause rose in recognition of the intuitive leadership and insight brought by women, I asked myself how many businesses actually allowed themselves to benefit from the natural leadership qualities of their female colleagues. Like birds that can sense the coming storm, female intuition, when well-developed, can help to circumnavigate business with clarity.

How often have we used the words "read between the lines" without realizing that not everyone can read intuitively? For most women, listening for hints in dialogue comes naturally, like breathing. This skill is a crucial factor in the success of female-led businesses. Yet, it seems more difficult for our male colleagues to demonstrate the same level of intuitive direction. Like owls, women possess the uncanny ability to view a situation from afar while making accurate predictions and preparations to capture the prey or protect the nest. Impactful business leaders like James Mwangi succeed by recognizing and harnessing such intuition to benefit the business and improve the economy.

A. Seek Enhanced Visioning

With leadership in business, it is true that intuition cannot be defined in scientific or financial terms. Still, each entrepreneur needs to understand the vision precisely and communicate the viewpoint clearly, leaving no room for ambiguity. Every entrepreneur needs the courage to do the unusual and patience to see the results. That clarity will be the foundation upon which a solid, attainable vision is built in the long term.

When I first met Madam Folorunsho Alakija, it was with a healthy curiosity to see what Africa's wealthiest woman was really about. She came off her private jet in a pair of jeans and a simple blouse, her wealth betrayed only by the mink thrown casually over her shoulders. She seemed quite comfortable with the cold, windy front at Boston's Logan Airport. We had waited over an hour for her: myself, Farai Gundan of Forbes, and Wendy Ajuwon, my former teammate at Samsung West Africa who had flown in from London to co-manage the MIT Africa conference with me.

We were not disappointed. Folorunsho Alakija turned out to be a kindly but shrewd businesswoman with a maternal gentleness to her touch. She laid both hands on my pregnant belly and prayed for the twins within, calling forth greatness upon them in the tradition of Yoruba mothers. It was the best first meeting ever as she acknowledged my work as a mother, ahead of my work as an academic and business professional. She saw the effort and commitment it took to arrange a summit about the progress of Africa while we were working from the diaspora. Over that long weekend, I learned to see business through the eyes of faith as she explained how she became wealthy by waiting for divine direction and intuitively sensing the perfect timing for key business decisions.

I learned that in the earlier days, when the Nigerian oil industry boomed newly, many people advised Folorunsho Alakija to sell or exploit her holdings. She would have made a very good profit then, but something told her to wait. With the same intuition Mary Wamae showed at Equity Bank, Folorunsho Alajika exercised restraint as she built other parts of her business empire while waiting for the right timing to exploit crude oil. Her decision turned out to be the ace that won the game. Decades after the initial rush to exploit, her oil holdings were ready to begin work, and the results are in the billions of dollars that have since proven her right.

As an entrepreneur, Madam Alakija understood timing, and she understood faith. Both are necessary for survival in business. Faith in oneself and the divinity of our collective purpose and faith in the timing of our efforts and actions to suit that purpose are necessary to succeed.

B. Owls Are Time-Conscious

Early bird calls wake us in the morning, and soothing bird songs calm us in the evening. Yet, many modern humans have come to associate the hoot of an owl with a premonition of danger. A bird knows when to fly south and how and when to return once the weather is warm again, yet the owl often remains in its home, whatever the weather. Timing is critical to the survival of avian species, with long distances covered just in time and preparations made before the seasons change. Yet, the owl thrives during seasons of scarcity and is able to find sustenance intuitively. This type of intuition is important in business and needs to be cultivated deliberately for effectiveness in leadership.

Owls are resourceful nesters: with an uncanny ability to make homes in several different types of environments, owls build nests in the hollows of trees, caves, ground holes, barns, and other structures. Some owls have been known to displace hawks, crows, and other large birds, claiming the nests as their new home. Unlike most other birds, owls are not weather migrators; they stay put in the same home throughout the year. Like owls, our investments should be profitable all year round, and equally, our vigilance should be all-encompassing.

We encourage women leaders to develop SMART goals for business growth and to review personal progress at regular intervals. Decide on weekly, monthly, quarterly, and yearly updates. Communicate progress to your mentor and team, and take deliberate steps to improve on past performances constantly.

C. Female Intuition Is Real

As women in leading roles, we need to use intuition as a business benefit because our teams will gain ground by leveraging this natural gift. It helps to write our observations and impressions down so that we can review them later. Note the main points and give the rationale in a way that is easy for everyone to understand. It is equally important to differentiate between microwave speed projects and slow-cooking special interest projects and use wisdom to balance both extremes when making strategic plans.

The myth of magic in female-led businesses is that women are able to harness their intuition in ways that move our markets forward and set example for others in our business ecosystem. Backed with evidence and supported by good strategy, intuition can make the difference between a business that survives the storm and one that thrives in the face of such challenges.

D. Understand the Purpose of Nests and Eggs

Listening to Thelma Ekiyor of She Works Here, an all-women accelerator in Nigeria, as she gave entrepreneurial advice to a cohort of businesswomen, I learned an important lesson for my own business growth. According to Ms. Ekiyor, women need to have "other streams of income that do not depend on the new business." She made it clear that a startup leader cannot realistically expect to live on the proceeds of a new business, so she advises that parallel income should be generated to minimize the stress and financial pressure. She gave examples of the minor streams of income in her portfolio and urged leaders to pre-invest in smaller, everyday income generators that would help them make ends meet if necessary.

The recent COVID-19 pandemic gave further weight to Thelma's advice as we witnessed the closure of some businesses which many believed to have been beyond failure. Many mentors advise women to build nest eggs for business expansion, education, and personal welfare, healthcare, or just for responding to emergencies. The widespread emergency of the coronavirus recession has been a global case study from which we all are still learning.

E. Learn Industrial Geography

As a woman in business, it is important to know how, where, and when business is done within your location and business setting. Information acquisition is key so that sound (and timely) business decisions can be made. Being sensitive to the winds of change, women in leadership can anticipate the likely outcomes of global events and proactively position their businesses to weather the storm and thrive where many others fail.

As it is taught in most faith-based belief systems, passion for the outcome translates to reward and fulfilment. In the same vein, passion encourages active growth along your chosen career or business path. We advise that business strengths, weaknesses, opportunities, and threats should be evaluated on a regular basis and reviewed to reflect the current realities of the marketplace.

The owl's 360-degree head turn allows it to see the terrain in totality. Similarly, business leaders need to have a panoramic view of the business ecosystem since the terrain is constantly shifting, and small businesses are often more seriously affected by changes in the local economy.

TIPS FROM MOTHER NATURE: Wowww like an Owl!

Remember to build a nest of smart investments.

Remember to learn the geography of your industry.

Remember to turn and explore new viewpoints.

Remember to embrace dark days and see them through by faith.

Remember that female intuition is a business benefit.

PRACTICE:
Intuitively identify three world events that could affect your work, and visualize your proactive response.

CHAPTER 8

Turtles: Manage Resources and Adapt

We have all heard the story of the hare and the tortoise. This well-known fable, attributed to Aesop, an ancient Greek writer, and later adapted by Jean de La Fontaine, tells the tale of a competition between the hare and the tortoise. It highlights essential lessons on perseverance, humility, and diligence. So, you might expect to read a paragraph on these three managerial qualities in this chapter. However, I want to draw your attention first to a popular image: that of the Woman Tortoise—the one who carries the world and everyone's problems on her back. I bet that reminds you of someone.

The tortoise and its shell are inseparable, contrary to what one might think. They are one and the same. If you find yourself feeling the weight of your family's problems, your colleagues' issues, and your personal troubles all becoming one, I invite you to adopt a shell to defend and protect yourself from anything that could harm your physical and mental well-being.

As a child, I adored the Teenage Mutant Ninja Turtles—Michelangelo, Leonardo, Raphael, and Donatello. Like my three brothers, they represented the masculine side of me, the part that fights to the last and uses its shell against any external threat. Growing up, I quickly realized that we live in a world where aggression is constant. Between clichés and preconceived ideas, becoming a woman who defends her values and opinions can be frowned upon, especially when one is at the head of an organization. So, almost instinctively, I imagine raising my shield whenever I face something that offends my morals or goes against my life principles. But I also learned to be content with what I had while hoping for better days.

I remember the time when, overnight, my father decided that I would no longer use the car and the driver, kindly inviting me to take the "car rapide," a form of public transport in Senegal known to be dangerous and a haven for pickpockets and all sorts of encounters. At first, I thought it was a joke until I realized he was serious. From quick rides in a 4x4, I transitioned to the slowness and multiple stops of public transport. I learned to manage my resources to avoid running out of money for my commute. More importantly, this experience taught me to adapt with patience and resilience.

A. Manage Your Resources

We all agree that the turtle is not the fastest animal on earth, yet it gets to its destination in one piece. It is wise to consider the strategy of the turtle as a mobile enterprise carried by the strength of self-motivation.

This reminds me of the informal businesses in Africa. Street vendors, also known as itinerant merchants, roam the streets of Dakar, from Colobane to Sandaga, carrying their goods in their arms, shouting at the top of their lungs, and sometimes competing creatively with joyful and quirky songs to attract customers.

Similar traditional business models, built on the analogy of the turtle, exist across West Africa. The Igbo Apprenticeship System in Nigeria is one such model, allowing younger entrepreneurs to learn and grow while relying on the guidance and resources provided by established operators. Over an agreed period of apprenticeship, the candidates graduate into fully-fledged businesses. They, in turn, take on several apprentices who become affiliates to the network of businesses ahead of them, thus populating the marketplace and serving a variety of related audiences.

This concept also inspired the On-Site Distributor Organization (OSDO) strategy we adopted when I was at Procter & Gamble. We established distributors in busy markets for ease of access rather than replenishing clients in hard-to-reach areas. Understanding the complexity of African markets, we maximized resources by using

OSDOs as branches of the leading distributor, with motorbikes navigating the winding streets for deliveries.

But as slow as the turtle may seem, there is comfort in knowing that it carries all its resources in one compact unit and thrives at its own pace. This model of resilience and adaptability is one we can all learn from.

B. Adapt Quickly and Be Flexible

Speaking of adaptability, turtles do not have teeth but still manage to chew their food, smell with their throats, and make the most of what they have to live very long lives. They can adapt to various situations, retreating into their shells when necessary. In Japan, turtles are seen as symbols of good fortune and longevity. I imagine I had to draw on this quality when, after a decade in the private sector, I decided to pursue a career in diplomacy.

Now, after 16 years of working as a professional, as I write these lines, I cannot fathom what I would have become if I had not been able to adapt personally and professionally to these two very different worlds. The decision-making processes, the speed of executing missions, and the importance of innovation are many factors that differ between them. But adapting also means continuous learning. So, just this past year, I invested my energy, time, and resources in attending prestigious institutions such as Harvard Business School, eCornell University, INSEAD (Institut Européen d'Administration des Affaires (European Institute of Business Administration)), HEC Montreal (École des Hautes Études Commerciales de Montréal (School of Higher Commercial Studies of Montreal)), and the University of Cambridge to hone my skills and enhance my abilities as an Innovation Officer. Continuous learning has become the door to career growth and ease of adaptation for me.

C. Nurture Your Resilience

Turtles belong to one of the oldest reptile groups globally, dating back to the time of the dinosaurs, over 200 million years ago. Their remarkable adaptability explains their enduring presence.

Similarly, turtles are often linked with longevity due to their long-term perspective. I believe that just like turtles, effective managers must prioritize long-term goals and strategic planning over short-term results.

In none of my predictions did I envision myself becoming the Senior Innovation Platform Officer for the African Development Bank, the premier financial institution supporting the continent. This is certainly not where I saw myself 10 years ago, but I always knew I would serve the continent in one way or another. This has been my focus throughout my career. What kept me awake at night has always been: "How can I make an impact and make this continent THE one."

Now, the courage it took to transition from the private sector, where I mainly supported governments in their journey to the digital economy, to the impressive world of diplomacy was immense. I had to shift my mindset multiple times to navigate the processes, team dynamics, and local realities. The most challenging aspect of my daily work—mobilizing resources with partners to support innovation and entrepreneurship across Africa—is infusing everything I learned at IBM, being a "wild duck," into a triple-A institution that follows certain rules and procedures. There was a time when I heard whispers referring to me as "the rebel." Although I was not fundamentally at odds with the rules, my entire career had conditioned me to make them more flexible to achieve business objectives. This has helped me build a sustainable future for both the team and the Innovation & Entrepreneurship Lab I am managing.

As a manager, persevering through challenges and consistently working towards long-term objectives has been crucial since I believe success typically stems from steady, continuous progress rather than quick, fleeting bursts of activity.

D. Protect Yourself

Whether on land or in water, the hard shell of a turtle poses a formidable challenge to predators, ensuring its safety. Just as turtles retreat into their shells for protection, we too can benefit from taking time to retreat and prioritize self-care. We can decide when and where we need to be with ourselves. This may involve carving out quiet moments for meditation, indulging in hobbies, or simply stepping away from the demands of daily life. Regular retreats allow us to recharge and sustain our well-being.

A turtle's shell serves as a natural protective barrier. Similarly, we can establish and uphold healthy boundaries to safeguard our mental and physical health. This includes learning to say NO to excessive commitments, avoiding toxic relationships, and allocating time and space for ourselves.

E. Take the Time It Needs to Get There

"Rome was not built in a day," and as a Senegalese proverb would say, "Haste and hurry can only bear children with many regrets along the way." In business, as well as in our personal lives, it is important to know when to wait and when to launch. While working on this book, Funké and I spent more than two and a half years navigating between professional and personal commitments, health challenges, and unexpected events. A good understanding of the times and the patience to wait can make the difference for just about every business. Remarkably, female turtles are very committed to procreation. They nurture their young over an extensive period while teaching them necessary life skills.

This commitment ensures that the next generation is able to thrive and continue independently. This lesson is important for us as we pay attention to continuity management in our work, ensuring that we mentor valuable young talents who will grow our industries and carry our collective hopes into the next generation.

TIPS FROM MOTHER NATURE: Be practical like a turtle!

Remember to manage your resources efficiently.

Remember to adapt to various circumstances by leaning in your abilities.

Remember to be resilient—learn to navigate out of your comfort zone.

Remember to protect yourself physically and mentally.

Remember to take the time needed to get to where you want to be.

PRACTICE:

Identify five ways to efficiently manage your resources and five steps to practice self-care.

CHAPTER 9

Lions: Stealth and Market Leadership

Good leadership involves clever management of mutual dependencies. The lioness needs the lion, as the lion needs the pride. Sensitive cultural situations require wisdom, and survival requires a willingness to see the common vision from different points of view. As lionesses in the business terrain, women need to understand the context of every meeting and anticipate the outcomes - whether these are desired or otherwise. Cultural sensitivity means being conscious of age, gender, tribal, or other unspoken issues that may affect the running of the business. Bearing the symbol of lioness, leading women must rise above psycho-social obstacles by constantly producing good work and consistently showing personal integrity.

Everyone respects a sound businesswoman. Even opponents and competitors grow to revere the astute female leader. Like the lioness, let your work and reputation speak positively for you. The Maasai Mara in Kenya and the Great Serengeti in Tanzania have given us an excellent opportunity to analyze the behavior of lions. We find that sometimes, the female may grow a mane resembling a male lion and lead the pride as a gender proxy. In some pride, two or more mother lionesses unite to lead and protect their territory. As in Nature, so it works in business. Wise female leaders learn to work with a gender proxy for the enhanced business interface when necessary.

A. Use Stealth Strategically

Binta Mohammed went to fashion school after working for years at her father's tailoring shop in Obalende, Lagos. Setting up her own shop in the swanky Ikeja area of the same city, it took a few months before people noticed the high-quality work she was doing. As the Muslim Eid festival approached, many women brought her blocks of fabric to sew into garments for their families. Mostly, the women asked her to please remove some yards of fabric for the man of the house. They took that portion to a man-tailor who made the husband's garment.

Binta was trained by the best man-tailor she knew, her father. She could also give her clients the ease of sewing all their Eid garments in one shop. However, the religious beliefs of her clientele did not allow for her (a woman) to take measurements that required touching the bodies of men. She could not yet afford to employ a man-tailor, but she needed to show her customers what she could do. She decided on a stealth plan.

In the weeks before Eid, Binta invested in fabric and made kaftans with fine embroidery, clothing her teenage son in a new one every day. She taught him how to take measurements and write down clients' choices in the shop register. As her female customers were dropped off by their husbands for fittings, Binta's son welcomed them and was admired by both the men and the women. To each admirer, the teenager suggested that he could take the man's measurements so that a similar or more detailed style could be made. The husband's garment would, of course, be delivered at the same time as the rest. All the teenager did was take measurements. Binta made the garments, and that one move grew her business exponentially.

B. Find Your Pride

The first unit of business success is the team. To make a good team, the leader must identify positive traits and trainable flaws in themselves, as well as in other members. To build the right team, women in business need to find voices that echo their visions while picking similarly lion-minded leaders to groom for the future of the team. Consider your team to be your first advantage, and leverage each ambassador as a source of confidence to your clients.

Having said that, selecting teammates who are different and diverse in their trajectories is equally important. This makes for a good mix of opinions and experiences on the team. A good team or pride is one where no member is afraid to roar, and each partakes in the hunting and the subsequent feasting.

C. Leverage Strength with Silence

In the African business environment, new ideas are fragile, and concepts need protection between incubation and market entry. As leaders handling issues that span sensitive aspects of life, women learn to use stealth as a timely shield during critical periods of business growth. Stealth often involves silence, which can be leveraged as a strategic tool in business.

While communication is key to perception management, silence is mandatory at certain points in the development of a business or concept. As women in leadership, we must learn when to share our projects internally and when to advertise our achievements externally. As the lionesses of the Maasai Mara and Serengeti know, silence is not the absence of activity.

D. Cooperate to Raise Generations

With lionesses, cubs are raised in common, and collective protection is given by pride members who defend the family or territory from outsiders. Grouping is a protective strategy that shelters new additions to the group. The same analogy works in business, where leaders must identify possible future leaders and strategically prioritize continuity management. For businesses to grow into cross-generational success stories, the incumbent leader must make it a point of duty to find, train, and equip the next line of leadership for the business.

Lionesses cooperate in the traditional African way by raising their cubs together in a collective of mothers overseeing the pride. By cooperating with one another, mutually protecting one another, and presenting a united front, these lionesses enlarge their territories and preserve the pride holdings for generations yet unborn. As the well-known adage goes, it takes a village to raise a child. I would add that it takes pride to raise a cub and a lioness-type leader to bring a multi-generational idea or concept to fruition.

E. Maintain Consistency to Establish Territory

As a pride rules over the territory and ensures the continuity of the generations to come, we also, as leaders in business, must be consistent in our values, insistent on our integrity, and persistent with our passion for the right outcomes to follow our efforts. By establishing our strengths and re-evaluating our positions, women are better able to defend the territory won by dint of hard work and by our investment across industries.

Although the lioness and the cat belong to the same greater animal family, they cannot be confused for one another because each one exhibits behaviors that are consistent with the character and the environment within which they exist. When we look at the pride of lions, we clearly see that other animals steer clear of the territory marked by lions because of the lions' reputation for territorial defense and intentional hunting. In the same vein, the character of a business is largely defined by the leaders and by the ideals and values to which these leaders subscribe.

TIPS FROM MOTHER NATURE: Lead like a lioness!

Remember to find the right members for your pride.

Remember to leverage stealth as a leadership strategy.

Remember that the lioness is active even when silent.

Remember to cooperate like lionesses for survival.

Remember, it takes consistency to establish territory.

PRACTICE:

List five territorial barriers to surmount in your work.

CHAPTER 10

Octopus: The Power of Emotional Intelligence

In 2002, when my father passed away, I felt like my entire world was collapsing. I was preparing for my Certificate of Completion of Middle Studies (BFEM) exam when, a month prior, my father, who had just returned from Mecca, fell gravely ill. His once-piercing gaze and strong physical presence were fading. I took care of him while preparing for the exam, studying with my books on my crossed legs, massaging his feet, and giving him his medication because we were very close. As the youngest of four and the only girl bearing my grandmother's name, he prayed for me constantly in his final days.

I will never forget the day I saw him in a wheelchair. I ran away to avoid seeing him so dependent. His illness worsened, and it became evident he knew he would not survive. We were more optimistic, hoping for his recovery. Only days or weeks after his passing did we realize that he was preparing us for the end through his cryptic messages, riddles, and moral lessons. We found his phone, unlocked, on the refrigerator in his room, with a message in Drafts, detailing the administrative procedures to follow in case of his death. It was undoubtedly for my mother, for whom he had great compassion, knowing she would be lost amid all this.

Why am I sharing this story? Because at that precise moment when I realized my father would no longer be by my side, I was utterly lost. Yet, I managed to find enough strength to rise above and achieve my goal of being at the top of my class, as I had promised him before he left us.

The truth is, it felt like I had three hearts. Perhaps it was the weight of the promise I had made, but I felt within me three different personalities guiding me toward a somewhat happy ending.

73

One heart grieved deeply, so much that I went to knock on my father's door the day after his death, still in shock and denial. The second heart stayed motivated, focusing on my goal and finding ways and strategies to reach my main goal - being the first in my Jury as I had promised my dad. The third heart empathized with my mother and brothers as I have always been the pillar of the family. Despite my young age, my opinions—perhaps more so than my brothers'—have always mattered, thanks to my father and our Lebou culture, where women play a significant role and lineage is matrilineal.

In the end, not only was I the 1st in my Jury, but I was also the best in the entire center. Again, why do I share this? Because without my "three hearts," I do not think I would have had the emotional intelligence and clarity to achieve my goal with such composure.

What's the connection with the octopus? Octopuses have three hearts—two that pump blood through the gills and a systemic heart that pumps blood to the entire body. I believe this creature symbolizes our ability to manage our emotions, with the heart being a central organ for humans.

A. Develop Your Emotional Intelligence

Having three hearts suggests a certain level of autonomy and flexibility. According to scientific research, octopuses can quickly adapt to different environments and situations, changing their color and texture to blend in with their surroundings and squeezing through tight spaces. As women leaders, I believe we also have the capabilities to adjust strategies and tactics in response to changing market conditions or organizational needs. This adaptability should also extend to our willingness to delegate tasks without fear or anxiety.

Additionally, octopuses possess eight arms and even have a preference for which arm they use for eating. Each arm can operate independently, allowing the octopus to multitask and respond quickly to stimuli. Similarly, in developing our businesses, we can implement a decentralized decision-making structure where team members are empowered to make decisions. This approach can enhance efficiency and responsiveness within the organization.

B. Focus and Strategize

You might know octopuses have nine brains—one central brain between their eyes and a mini-brain in each arm. They can even regenerate lost limbs, demonstrating incredible resilience in the face of adversity. This teaches us that we can embrace recovery and growth after setbacks. One key lesson I have learned from my 16 years of professional experience and overcoming challenges is the importance of resourcefulness. It is crucial to make the best use of available resources and foster a culture of innovation and ingenuity.

Furthermore, when hunting, octopuses exhibit remarkable focus and precision in their movements. We, too, should aim for precision and focus in executing our strategies and tasks, ensuring that our efforts are directed towards achieving specific, measurable goals.

C. Solve Problems by Communicating Clearly

Octopuses are renowned for their problem-solving abilities; they are among the few animals capable of using tools and solving puzzles to obtain food. They also use camouflage not only for protection but also for communication by signaling intentions to others. As women in business, this encourages us to cultivate our skills, fostering creative thinking and innovative solutions to overcome challenges. Like octopuses, we should excel in effective communication, ensuring messages are clear and tailored to different audiences. This also involves being transparent and fostering an open communication environment.

D. Be Authentic

Octopuses have another fascinating trait: they have blue blood. The protein haemocyanin, which transports oxygen in the octopus's body, uses copper instead of iron found in our own haemoglobin. This copper-based protein is more efficient at carrying oxygen molecules in cold and low-oxygen conditions, making it ideal for oceanic life. This uniqueness serves as a reminder that we, too, are distinctive in our ways of thinking, acting, and managing both difficult and ordinary situations. It is our responsibility to nurture this authenticity by surrounding ourselves with individuals who appreciate our differences. Therefore, it's crucial that we prioritize continuous learning and development for ourselves and our teams, fostering a culture of intellectual growth and curiosity.

E. Motherhood Is a SuperPower

When I was pregnant with my son Hamid, I constantly craved octopus—I know this is super weird—even though it wasn't as readily available in Côte d'Ivoire as it is back home in Senegal. I often wonder if that's why I found myself multitasking so much when he was born. Having undergone breast surgery earlier in life, I didn't produce enough milk for his voracious appetite, so I had to pump constantly to meet his needs. It made me realize that as we juggle work, feeding, healing, changing, playing, cleaning, caring, and teaching, mothers are like octopuses with eight arms. While female octopuses also juggle between eating and caring for their eggs, by the time their eggs hatch, female octopuses are either dying or dead. Now, we surely don't have to sacrifice ourselves in the same way; instead, I've come to understand that our ability to multitask is a strength that extends beyond motherhood and into our professional lives. It's one of the reasons why women excel in business—they're naturally adept at managing multiple responsibilities simultaneously.

One day, while catching up on sleep and preparing for a meeting, I asked my mom how she managed with three boys and a girl. While having a supportive husband makes a difference, she recognized that our generation faces different challenges compared to our mothers'. Fortunately, innovative minds have developed applications that help facilitate the lives of modern moms.

Being a mom, in general, isn't easy. Still, it's a most rewarding and fulfilling role, and it best encapsulates the very nature of creation. Like Mother Nature, women embrace the unique ability to juggle several aspects of life in perfect harmony.

TIPS FROM MOTHER NATURE: Enhance your EQ like an octopus!

Remember to develop your emotional intelligence.

Remember to strategize to get to where you want to be.

Remember to focus on finding ways to solve problems.

Remember to be authentic in your unique way when building your personality.

Remember that parenting also builds your soft skills.

PRACTICE:

Identify five ways to develop your emotional intelligence.

CHAPTER 11

Elephants: Wisdom and Information

Early in life, elephants learn the routes that lead to food sources, guaranteeing the continued survival of their species. Elephants understand seasonalities and natural changes. They also understand geographical landmarks, ancient paths, and watering hole locations. Similarly, in business today, technological advancements have made it easier to go digital for convenient vision setting, growth planning, and review progress over time. Winning involves using the information that is freely available and learning as much as possible about the business and industry.

Like the female-led elephant herds, strong organizations keep proper records of leadership decisions, learned lessons, and new discoveries. In light of the rapidly changing environment, it is wise to have Memoranda of Understanding (MOUs) and contracts in place, and to ensure that all contract terms are well understood before committing to them. Once these have been established, good leaders ensure integrity in the execution of contract terms and provide guidance to the team in case things do not go as anticipated.

A. Listen to Experts

During the COVID-19 pandemic lockdown in Kenya, many businesses witnessed the kind of turmoil that is rarely experienced on a global scale. Nonetheless, each person, household, and enterprise had to deal with it. While moderating a webinar with a wide international audience, I asked one of the panelists what single piece of advice she would give to entrepreneurs at that point in time. In a serious tone, the panelist Fatma El-Maawy emphasized her words with care. She was speaking to women entrepreneurs listening in from across Africa, with a specific interest in the female leaders doing business in Kenya. As the Second Vice President of Kenya National Chamber of Commerce and Industry, she had an insider's perspective on the realities of business scaling, funding and partnerships, capacity building, and growing stimulation within the market. Her response to the question: if there is one piece of advice you could give to female entrepreneurs, what would it be?

"Formalize your business, and join advocacy groups that support your industry." Her reply had no ambiguity, and that sage advice has remained with me ever since.

To attract growth and much-needed funding for entrepreneurial startups, women need to formalize their business operations and present their growing concern as a recognized legal entity. Many entrepreneurs make the mistake of waiting to scale before registering their businesses formally or having auditable accounts and processes. A business is not a recognized entity until it is registered as such by the government of the day within the governing policies and regulations that define the market. Without formal registration, entrepreneurs cannot benefit from the advantages of the chambers of commerce and industry or participate in accessing more formal financing options like grants, which were made available for MSMEs (Micro, Small, and Medium Enterprises) through the African Development Bank.

Women need to understand the seasons of business, the periods of funding, and the reality of resources that are available to them. It is good practice to keep records of all financial transactions and have audit-friendly cash policies in place from the onset. More importantly, we advise separating personal expenditures from business spending and keeping records separate to allow easier auditing and due diligence.

B. Outsource the Extras

Experienced leaders advise enterprise starters to find experts who can do things that are beyond the core competence of the owner-manager. Proper legal assistance, accurate accounting, and auditing processes help to give credibility to a growing business. There are resources to help find such experts who work for MSMEs at reduced rates. With outsourced services, the entrepreneur has more time to focus on the core business while entrusting those specialized areas to experts.

The importance of advocacy groups cannot be overemphasized at this point in the growth of a business. By joining forces with like-minded people, we increase our chances of success with the bigger agenda. When these advocacy group memberships are leveraged correctly, shared experiences often lead to shared solutions since most are facing similar challenges. The members can thus benefit from economies of scale when they join forces. As it is unusual to see a lone elephant, we understand from this great force of nature that wisdom resides in the herd, and leadership is optimized by the longevity of vision. The elephant who leads the herd is often the eldest female and one who knows the secrets of group survival.

C. Practice Long-Haul Mentoring

In 1929, the women of Aba in eastern Nigeria set off a chain of riots that caused huge ripples in the colonial business of West Africa. The women activists succeeded in affecting legislation, leadership positions, and the administration of colonial governance. They also won the right NOT to be further impoverished by paying tax for merchandise dealt on the open market. This movement spread through the rural market networks and had a massive impact across West Africa.

Today, women doing business across Africa need to understand the kind of strength that comes from remembering the victories of our forebears. Like the memory of an elephant, cross-generational history helps the next leaders learn from previous ones. An unbreakable chain of wisdom is preserved and bequeathed through the line for the good of the entire group.

Remarkably, when one elephant leader passes, she passes on the wealth of knowledge to a younger one who has been trained to find the sources of food and water to help the herd survive in difficult times. Knowing the route and surviving the drought depends on the new leader's ability to learn from the activities (and mistakes) of the leaders before her. Mother Nature has conditioned these magnificent creatures to traverse the land with photographic memory and process accuracy. It is the perfect example of mentoring for cross-generational survival.

It is important to take mentoring seriously as women in leadership. Over time, the growth of both mentor and mentee will benefit the business and help to raise a stronger, more deliberate crop of female leaders across the continent. By teaching the young, we ensure that positive ideals and useful tips survive from one business generation to another.

D. Leverage Impressive Size

An elephant is more than the presence of one trunk. The Yoruba proverb says an elephant is beyond being described as a fleeting experience. It is fundamental that women in business learn to leverage the size of our combined networks and use this to benefit our businesses, careers, families, and national economies. One elephant is a thing of wonder, but a herd of elephants is simply awe-inspiring. The sound of unified purpose can be heard for miles as smaller players dart away to avoid the stampede that we are able to generate with our collective strength.

During the old exploration days, across the African heartland, elephant riders astounded the audience by demonstrating how much weight an elephant could carry and how much good sense the elephant has. Similarly, as female leaders, we can carry a great deal of managerial weight and display the discipline and fortitude that helps to win in business and life.

E. Make Some Noise

The elephant does not pass quietly along the way but announces her presence with the drumbeats of her heavy footfalls and the trumpeting of her impressive trunk. As the activities of our minds are built around our plans for the future, which include the success of our businesses, we must be conversant with the kind of footprints we are leaving and the kind of noise we are making. In much the same manner as elephants, marketing communication will make the right announcement at the right place if timed for the highest effect. Women leaders must understand the timing of marketing and the reasons for each activity that ties into the business at hand.

I am quick to tell my students that a short course does not a marketing expert make, but with experience and guidance, intuitive entrepreneurial marketing is possible for business leaders. There are many opportunities to learn how best to make marketing noise, and there are avenues for accessing high-quality marketing output on a frugal startup budget. The wisdom of the elephant is built on knowledge that is inherited and then used for the good of all. This is the way leadership should look at systemic mentoring.

TIPS FROM MOTHER NATURE: Be memorable like an elephant!

Remember to relate and boldly tell your own story.

Remember to learn from the experiences of others.

Remember to find mentors for long-term survival.

Remember to leverage network size for protection.

Remember to make some good (marketing) noise!

PRACTICE:
List five business achievements that you can leverage to make some noise.

CHAPTER 12

Camels: Keep Walking, Keep Saving

The camel is the ultimate travel companion across the sands of North Africa. Able to conserve water while covering hundreds of desert miles, the camel offers both safety and a good vantage point for its riders. In business and personal endeavors, the ability to outlast competitors through preparation and sheer determination is crucial for survival. Additionally, being useful to others within our immediate environment facilitates collective survival, thus further protecting our interests. The camel remains calm during droughts, and when it reaches a water source, it retains as much as possible. Those who learn from the camel will store excess resources and muster the courage to endure long stretches of scarcity.

This reminds me of my first camel ride in Abu Dhabi, United Arab Emirates. Taking advantage of a weekend while covering the Middle East, Africa, and Turkey, I decided to enjoy the desert excursions offered by local agencies. From thrilling Jeep rides across the sand dunes to the slow pace of the camel, I experienced the varied facets of my career at IBM—extremely intense marketing campaign preparations for sales teams followed by quiet periods when colleagues go on holiday in July and August. What struck me the most was gently tapping my feet, urging the camel to move faster, as I found its pace too slow. I was losing patience.

A. Savings Require Resilience

The camel is a universal symbol of resilience. It can drink up to 20 gallons of water at once, storing it in its bloodstream and allowing it to endure long periods without water. Similarly, African women have learned to be resilient during challenging times by saving money and pooling resources for the benefit of their families and businesses. Having a rainy-day fund is essential, as is investing for future gains. Nowadays, even those unfamiliar with the stock market can learn to invest using online platforms. The most important first step is to start with small savings and gradually increase them, transforming this practice from a hobby into a valuable skill.

B. Long-term Vision

Camels are adapted to survive in extreme environments by planning for long journeys across deserts. Similarly, in business, adopting a long-term perspective on savings and investments ensures sustainable growth and stability, preparing the organization for future challenges. My first experience with saving began at age 10 when my mother showed me her "money box." At the time, I laughed, not realizing that this was her savings, which she later broke open to buy me a denim that I still remember vividly. That outfit is unforgettable to me, not because of its cost but because of the gesture behind it. I promised myself to work harder than ever that year at school, recognizing the sacrifice my mother made by breaking her savings.

Effective financial management involves conserving resources during prosperous times to ensure availability during lean periods, highlighting the importance of building a financial cushion for unexpected expenses.

C. Setting Priorities

Camels maximize the efficiency of their stored resources, using them sparingly and wisely. Similarly, businesses can optimize their financial resources by prioritizing essential expenditures and avoiding unnecessary costs, thus maximizing the value derived from every saving. Prioritization can be a significant challenge for many, and a colleague once remarked that "the only thing we know how to prioritize is the inevitable."

It was during the COVID-19 pandemic that I truly grasped the power of prioritizing. Living alone in an apartment in Abidjan, I had to be methodical about the type of purchases I made and the quantities

I stocked to ensure I had vital supplies during the uncertain times of the pandemic. Moreover, there was no uncertainty as to what the money at the bank would become. We thought of another 2008 crisis; it was worse than that, but the unknown made it look less apocalyptic.

Creating shopping lists helped me become more pragmatic when I became a mother. I started using a budgeting app to track expenses and began buying in bulk. This disciplined approach allowed me to save significantly on monthly groceries and utilities. Instead of going out at least three times a week, I ordered online, benefiting from marketing coupons and promotional sales. This not only saved money but also conserved time and energy.

D. Cultivate Patience

One thing I continue to practice is patience. In a world where we are constantly moving at breakneck speed, we can learn much from the camel, which symbolizes the virtues of patience and perseverance. It teaches us to remain steadfast in our pursuits and not give up, even when things get tough.

In 2023, I launched two personal projects that, in my humble opinion, helped me develop patience. The first project is the SERENDIPITY planners, which are tools I designed based on training sessions I conducted and feedback from participants to help them focus on their strengths and be more productive. The planners come in three volumes, dividing the year into three sets of four months. They allow users to review their daily progress against morning objectives, weekly goals, and monthly targets. To my surprise, nearly 200 units were sold in the first year. Writing the quotes and developing these tools required sacrificing many hours of rest and weekends to write 365 quotes for each day of the year.

The second project is related to spirituality–SPIRITU'ELLES, a series of podcasts that connect Hadiths and concepts developed in the light of the Quran with personal development principles. The time spent recording and editing the various contributions–including

Quranic passages—and interacting with the audience in nearly 40 countries around the world made me realize that I am indeed capable of taking the time to do things well.

Moreover, I learned that just because something takes time does not mean it is a failure. I had to adjust my schedule to ensure I got enough sleep, as I worked mostly between 3 a.m. and 5 a.m., waiting for the Fajr prayer. Consequently, I had to go to bed earlier to balance my commitments and priorities.

E. Keep Calm

Camels remain calm under extreme stress, efficiently utilizing their stored resources to survive. Similarly, businesses should develop strategies for managing financial stress, such as diversifying investments and creating emergency funds, to ensure stability during economic downturns. This reminds me of Elsa, a school teacher I met at the airport during a trip within Africa. We were emerging from the darkest days of the pandemic, and nearly every business was struggling with the unpredictability and prolonged nature of the crisis. To my surprise, Elsa shared that she diversifies her investments across stocks, bonds, and real estate.

She explained that her revelation came after reading Robert Kiyosaki's book "Rich Dad, Poor Dad." Enthralled by its insights, she ended up buying and devouring almost all of his books within a month. As a result, during the economic downturn, her diversified portfolio helped mitigate losses, allowing her to maintain financial stability without significant stress. She still keeps the receipts for those books, calling them her smartest investment in years, as they enabled her to multiply her revenues and even plan ahead for her retirement.

TIPS FROM MOTHER NATURE: Save like a camel.

Remember that saving demands resilience.

Remember to embrace a long-term vision.

Remember to master the art of prioritizing.

Remember to nurture patience.

Remember to keep calm in all circumstances.

PRACTICE:
List five areas where your business can make some savings.

CHAPTER 13

Butterflies: Change Means Process

During a marketing class exercise at E4Impact Kenya, Mkamboi Mwakale, founder of Saru Organics, keyed in on the importance of co-branding partnerships and digital media leveraging. By deliberately partnering with complementary products, premium brands, and public personalities, the organic hair product brand is using in-kind exchanges to leverage the saturated marketplace and create a good buzz. Within 3 years, Saru Organics has gone from being a new entrant to being featured on the BBC and gaining international attention.

Like the iconic butterfly, the process of metamorphosis has seen Saru Organics re-invented through premium quality packaging, celebrity endorsements, and digitally expressed Afrocentric ideals in haircare. By staying true to the founding vision of using wholesome organic ingredients only while exploring new ways of meeting the needs of African customers, the brand has built a reputation for quality natural products using moringa, shea butter, tea tree, and other natural ingredients.

A. Embrace Digital Technology

The efficacy of the Saru Organics campaign is seen in the digital footprint of the brand, with online followers and news mentions that validate the claim to beautify "one African crown at a time." The ingenuity here is that Mkamboi has achieved such a high share of voice without a big advertising budget. Zero-budget marketing was one of the key outcomes of the marketing class, and Mkamboi was quick to adapt her go-to-market strategy to fit into the new learning. By creatively curating her digital campaign, the entrepreneur in Mkamboi was able to conserve funds, improve processes, and increase production capacity, which led to an increase in sales revenue and improvements in the customers' perceptions of quality. Mkamboi was growing her business by leveraging her network for mutually beneficial partnerships.

In the early days of business, the more successful leaders learn to use funds wisely. Where possible, we advise small businesses to barter products and services instead of paying cash. Volatile African markets compel many entrepreneurs to look to more developed economies for foreign direct investment, which usually does not come until the business has scaled to a certain point. Leveraging allows African entrepreneurs to find points of connection between the complementary local competencies and international market demands.

Across all industries and endeavours, good work attracts positive attention. As a leader in business, it is important to take the time to learn how to achieve more while spending less without compromising on quality and customer satisfaction. Successful leaders avoid cutting corners because the short-term gains swallow up the long-term benefits of being thorough in business.

The caterpillar needs the leaf to feed on, so it attaches itself to the plant and grows from within a silk cocoon. It is important to locate your business within easy reach of the customer base and near the source of materials. The logistics and process of operations must go hand-in-hand with the development planning, which is a necessary ingredient for success.

Socially speaking, the caterpillar can be classified as a loner, while the full-grown butterfly is seen as a more social persona—a groupie. The caterpillar becomes the butterfly only after a period of uncomfortable change processes. The outcome is a well-formed, beautiful, winged creature, unfettered by the limitations of its former caterpillar state. Similarly, businesses morph into more efficient versions of themselves when leaders understand the changes and seasons that make such changes necessary.

B. Practice Flexible Transformation

When the time for transformation comes, it is always more effective if the foundation is purpose-built to accommodate turnkey changes. Knowing that a natural haircare product would be expected to contain no artificial ingredients, chemical preservatives, or scents, Mkamboi planned to strategically optimize the product packaging. The ideological positioning of Saru Organics also affects the blend of ingredients and the type of packaging that will keep contents fresh and appealing to the user. The transformation from plastic cups to upcycled tubes should come as a natural follow-up to the green, planet-friendly persona of the brand.

Transformation can come in different forms, with varying reasons for the necessary change in operational processes. Transformation is a strength because we can use the improved competencies to grow our business concerns further. Positive transformation is the pathway to business growth. It is not surprising that butterflies travel farther than caterpillars, attract better goodwill than caterpillars, and are able to gather where caterpillars cannot.

C. Discipline at Incubation

Most entrepreneurs want to see progress within a short time, and decisions are made with the primary intention of increasing sales revenue. We advise new businesses and new extensions of established businesses to give enough time for incubating. When the caterpillar enters the cocoon stage, it is forced to stay still and grow into the change that is coming. This natural process occurs within a specific period and achieves a complete transformation of the caterpillar while it remains out of sight of possible predators.

The emerging creature becomes a thing of beauty, having passed through the struggle of cocooning and breaking free into full adulthood. If corners are cut and the cocoon is slit open without the struggle, the butterfly emerges crippled and deformed, its wings deprived of the strength that would have come out of the push to break free of the cocoon. It is expedient that management recognizes the cocooning period as an essential part of the growth process with businesses.

D. Swarming Is Good Leadership

Beyond the brilliant colours and poetic honours, when butterflies fly together in a swarm, they collectively feed by absorbing nutrients and salts from the soil around them. This dramatic natural activity also attracts legendary environmental attention, leading to the protection of certain species of butterflies. Applied to women in business, it is clear that our gatherings are of benefit to groups and individuals alike.

Women are better able to cross-pollinate ideas when working as a group. Therefore, we advise that female-led businesses invest in power networking so that leadership tips can be given and experiences can be shared with one another.

TIPS FROM MOTHER NATURE: Believe like a butterfly!

Remember good locations: caterpillars need leaves to live.

Remember seasonalities: change comes in every season.

Remember to be ready: have a flexible working strategy.

Remember to incubate properly: the cocoon serves a good purpose.

Remember to swarm: there is beauty in butterfly gatherings.

PRACTICE:
List five co-branding partnerships that can promote your work.

CHAPTER 14

Giraffes: Foresight for Continuity

Our symbol of foresight is the African giraffe—unique in height, physical build, and intelligence. Like these awe-inspiring creatures, the African woman leads with foresight, using her vantage position to scan the horizon for signs and to determine a better, safer future. The giraffe has nature's canvas smoothed over her form as skin. It allows her to blend in with the foliage in the savannah landscape, and she enjoys a competitive advantage by reaching the juicier leaves near the tops of trees.

A. Look Farther Ahead

When coronavirus hit the world economy in 2020, Africa's luxury brands took the biggest hit. Frugality became a necessity even for the elite, and luxury gave way to functionality. For one Kenyan brand, turning around meant putting the same high-quality production strategy into making stylish, protective face masks. Jeilo Collections' CEO Grace Mbugua was my guest on the female entrepreneurship webinar series *Impacting Women*, and we discussed business turnaround tactics for surviving the pandemic. She said it took faith and commitment to keep the machines running and the staff working.

Six months later, two new brand extensions had grown from that singular experience. Across the continent, women were beginning to earn money from sewing face masks, and a whole new segment of garment-making was born. The exposure also won new clients for Jeilo's luxury accessories line, which was revived once the lockdown was lifted.

B. Eat from Taller Trees

If the pandemic has taught us one thing in Africa, it is that we need cash reserves and strong, nimble strategies so that small businesses can survive such unexpected downturns. The absence of safety nets and the often inadequate business support policies make it difficult for entrepreneurs to weather the bigger storms. Like Grace Mbugua, the more resilient entrepreneurs use foresight to look beyond the immediate uncertainties and plot a way forward for the business.

The giraffe has access to foliage that is beyond most animal's reach. As business leaders, winners identify such systemic advantages and leverage those in times of need. There are advantages to be gleaned within our challenging environment and strong leaders are able to leverage such advantages. The relative affordability of labor, the relative ease of market penetration, the inclusive socio-economic policies, and the willingness for long-term mentoring are all opportunities that can be converted into business strengths.

C. Be Sensitive to Predators

Growth naturally attracts attention, and attention often includes predatory interest. As leaders learning from the giraffe in nature, we must remain sensitive to predatory activity and use our long-term vision to differentiate inclusiveness from deceptiveness.

Financial inclusion is needed to grow rural innovations into viable national profit makers, and wisdom with foresight is needed to carry these innovations onto the global stage. In the wild terrain where businesses compete for attention and compensation, it is important for leaders to be sensitive to the information given and to understand the intentions of potential competitors or commercial predators.

By leaning on mentors and leveraging group advocacy, many business leaders are able to use the systemic foliage for cover as they grow into independent market entities while staying out of sight and out of reach of predatory activity.

D. Be Ready to Blend In

Despite the height of a giraffe, it takes an experienced eye to see it when feeding in certain settings. The ability to eat while camouflaged amidst foliage gives the giraffe a safe spot when hiding in plain sight.

Immersion and acceptance are an undeniable part of growth when doing business in communities where goodwill counts towards project success. The host community thus becomes a protective space for the business to grow since it is seen as an integral part of the ecosystem.

When we blend in with the rest of the community, we are protected by the foliage of our ecosystem and assisted in times of difficulty. Stealth in the form of a natural camouflage is a gift from Mother Nature to the giraffe, whose ambling gait often cannot outrun a determined predator. By becoming one with the leaves and trees in the backdrop of the great open savannah, giraffe-type leaders are able to use their vantage points and camo-cover to the advantage of the business.

E. Expect the Unexpected

Decades ago, the CEO of Showers Books, Yomi Ogunlari, taught me how to make five- to ten-year plans for my personal and professional growth. She also taught me to leave room for unforeseen circumstances that might affect the achievement of my goals and to prepare alternative paths to my desired outcomes. That lesson has carried me far and proven invaluable in my career.

In the years that have passed since, I have watched as Grandma Books (as she is fondly called here) grew Showers from a greeting card-making print shop to a producer of educational books and reading materials which are now used across the Nigerian curriculum. As we prepare for the rollout of Showers books in East Africa, I remember the days of goal-setting and pre-planning, seeing the result of strategic leadership and continuous learning in the trans-generational growth of that company.

Most business leaders have not had training preparing them to contend with global phenomena at the scale of this novel coronavirus pandemic. Yet, in each case, we have all had to deal with the fallout and grow despite the setbacks. This is the evidence of resilience visible in all the businesses that have survived. The past following years are a testament to the resilience of businesses managed in our generation and a symbol of optimism about our ability to manage the coming years of global economic recovery successfully.

TIPS FROM MOTHER NATURE: Grow like a giraffe!

Remember to look ahead and see beyond your competition.

Remember to eat from the taller trees: leverage your advantage.

Remember to look out for predators within your ecosystem.

Remember to blend in and use your camouflage when needed.

Remember to be prepared: expect the unexpected.

PRACTICE:
Look ahead and list five milestones for your five-year plan.

CHAPTER 15

Conclusion: Even the Cactus Can Make a Forest

What is special about our house in Abidjan is that there are no flowers at the entrance; we have cactuses instead. I am sure many of our neighbors are wondering why I care so much about these strange plants. In fact, I am fascinated by their resilience. Have you ever wondered how the cactus survives in the desert? The cactus waits until nightfall to open its pores and capture carbon dioxide. The plant then waits for the sunrise to transform the captured carbon dioxide into carbohydrates that nourish the plant.

We women also have this ability. In difficult times, we women are naturally able to make ourselves look so beautiful that no one would suspect we are carrying untold burdens. It is the same for women in entrepreneurship. There will be moments of great success as well as periods of doubt and serious self-questioning. Like the cactus, we must not forget that we are capable of overcoming any obstacles that may come our way. You will need to understand and identify the constraints of your business environment and choose the strategy that will allow you to preserve your resources and take better advantage of any difficult situations. Like the cactus, we can flourish even in hostile environments.

On the other side of Africa, at Hellsgate National Park in central Kenya, a natural geothermal miracle makes the earth around the city of Naivasha behave differently. The lake sits majestically on one side, and the forest of cactus trees commands respect on the other (more mountainous) terrain, with deep canyons, rock towers, and gorges burping up steam from the earth. The terrain is ruggedly beautiful, not for the fainthearted and not for the feebler trees.

In a similar manner, the harsh business terrain notwithstanding, Africa is able to produce some of the world's most ingenious business ideas. Like the desert that grows the cactus, and like the cactus that makes a forest in the bare savannah, businesswomen are able to thrive in harsh conditions by leveraging the diversity of our products and progressing into new markets through deliberate cooperation that opens up the continent for increased regional trade.

In the course of these chapters, Absa and I have tried to show how like-minded leaders can share learnings that help us grow better together. We have learned five memorable lessons from Mother Nature after each chapter. Those reminders point us to the next step in our leadership journey. To put the learnings from this book into practice, we advise readers to create working documents from the activity points raised in each chapter. Put together, the ideation activities in each chapter lead to an aggregated self-improvement strategy that also benefits the community. We advocate that business leaders make recognizable contributions that generate goodwill within the wider industry. This will help with leveraging and co-branding for further growth and visibility and serve as an investment in goodwill within that community.

Lastly, while we have written this book from the perspective of the African woman, it is important to note that we have benefitted immensely from the support of men who believe in the abilities of women, and this has greatly enriched both our personal and professional lives. We have also had the privilege of learning from scenarios where our African background had to be adapted for new situations, with the support of non-Africans within our teams. This potential for wide application makes wisdom a shareable tool across communities.

We, therefore, advocate cultivating strong, diverse cross-community relationships and recognizing the importance of referees and local influencer partners. Good leadership has the same profitable outcome across all human communities. Regardless of gender, age, and culture, humans respond intuitively to positive stimuli and identify well with the source. It is our sincere hope that by sharing our experiences with nuggets of wisdom from Mother Nature, we all might do better as custodians of the dawning future.

TIPS FROM MOTHER NATURE: Thrive like the cactus!

Remember to dig deep and establish roots in fertile soil.

Remember to determine to succeed where others fail.

Remember to seek out like-minded stakeholders around you.

Remember to leverage structural similarities for mutual benefit.

Remember to occupy defendable territory with a working plan.

PRACTICE:

List five goals to achieve from the five-year plan you have now made.

References

Blewett, B.C. (2024). How to Avoid Strangers on Airplanes: Survival Guide for the Frequent Business Traveler (Hardback). http://booklife. com/project/how-to-avoid-strangers-on-airplanes-97679

Dutta, S & Parahoo, S & Afzal, M.N. & Harvey, H. (2021). A conceptual understanding of entrepreneurial motivation, employment creation, and supporting factors on micro-, meso- and macro-level entrepreneurship. World Review of Entrepreneurship, Management and Sustainable Development. 17. 56. 10.1504/WREMSD.2021.112093.

Eastman, K. and Laird, P. (1984) Teenage Mutant Ninja Turtles. Comics: Book I (Trade Paperback) Mirage Studios #1-3.

Holy Bible. Proverbs 6:6. NKJV. Reference to Solomonic verse on sluggards and ants.

Holy Quran. Surah An-Naml (The Ant), verses 18 and 19.

Kiyosaki, R. T. (2017). Rich dad poor dad (2nd ed.). Plata Publishing.

La Fontaine, J. D., Croxall, S. & Aesop. (1925) The fables of Aesop, text based upon La Fontaine and Croxall [Chicago, A. Whitman & Co].

Michaels, F. (2018). Sustainable Development in Sub-Saharan Africa: the Role of Intermediate State Powers in Economic Growth. (ITALIAN) PRIMO PIANO SULL'AFRICA: Lo sviluppo sostenibile nell'Africa sub-sahariana: EQUILIBRI. Milan, Italy. Edition 2 2018. https://www. rivisteweb.it/doi/10.1406/91689

Sydow, A. and Michaels, F. (2021) Female Entrepreneurship in Rural Kenya - Frugal Innovation within Tribal Constraints. ESCP Impact

Paper No 2021-39-EN. June 2021. https://academ.escpeurope.eu/pub/IP%202021-39-EN.pdf

Wasserman, E. A., Hugart, J. A., & Kirkpatrick-Steger, K. (1995). Pigeons show same-different conceptualization after training with complex visual stimuli. Journal of Experimental Psychology: Animal Behavior Processes, 21(3), 248–252. https://doi.org/10.1037/0097-7403.21.3.248

Mentions (In Order Of Appearance)

Foluke Kamson
Nike Alabi
Mimi Owodunni
Timi Deinsa-Adamolekun
Bolade Badmus
Kehinde Bademosi
Abraham Ninan
Reuben Onwubiko
Ken Nwachukwu
Oare Ojeikere
Yinka Akande
Sedi Inwutube
Segun Aina
Odunlami Kola-Daisi
Tunji Sobodu
Bayo Odeyale
Kehinde Akinsanya
Richard Ogunmodede
Pat Faniran
Kunbi Ademiluyi
Nella Nsa
Seun Omoyele-Dawodu
Timi Fischer
Sola Lawson
Ireke Amoji
Beverly Spencer-Obatoyinbo
Chika Osueke
Dele Ajayi
Uche Unigwe
Damian Nwatarali
Emmanuel Imoaghene
Yewande Adunola Ajuwon
Etelka Prosper

Mayena Barbara Chery
Rachel Merisier
Rachel Pratt
Hugline Jerome
Lyndia Dupre
Brad Bwasley Lovelace
Taylor Quarles
Victor Adebayo
Mame Diarra Gueye
Anass Moutaouakil
Ifeoma Okafor
Jean Paul Bom
Jamel Amoakoh Brown
Mathilda Wallace
Kevin Hawkins
Neil Comerford
Standa Vecera
Fadumo Dayib
Deborah Bailey
Vedette Gavin
Phyllis Johnson
Daniel Kipilosh
Ginni Rometty
Thomas J. Watson Sr.
Søren Kierkegaard
James Mwangi
Mary Wangari Wamae
Folorunsho Alakija
Farai Gundan
Thelma Ekiyor
Binta Mohammed
Fatma El-Maawy
Mkamboi Mwakale
Grace Mbugua
Yomi Ogunlari
Nana Benz group   (Historical advocacy group)
Queen Abla Pokou   (Historical figure)

About the Authors

Funké Nnennaya Michaels is an MIT Sloan Fellow and a Mason Fellow at Harvard University. First featured on Nigerian national TV with wisdom-based recitals from early childhood, Funké finds cultural bridges between businesses and host communities. With over 25 years spent in marketing, she is also a lecturer, public speaker, culture coach, and agricultural entrepreneur in East Africa. Funké lives on a reclaimed farm, travels the world, and enjoys the pleasures of a simple life and a large family.

@funkemichaels

Ndeye Absa Gningue is a diplomat and a dynamic African entrepreneur with over 16 years of experience. A tech enthusiast and passionate advocate for youth empowerment, she has built a stellar career in multinational sales and marketing strategy. Ndeye expertly bridges African culture with modern business practices. She leads JEADER, an NGO supporting young entrepreneurs across multiple countries, with a focus on empowering women entrepreneurs and expanding their reach through business partnerships. She is also the founder of ABC - Love Africa. Wear Africa, a fashion brand dedicated to promoting African creative industries.

@ndeyeabsagningue

Join us for an Exclusive Webinar!

Are you passionate about leadership and personal growth? Don't miss this opportunity to learn from two incredible thought leaders, **Funke Nnennaya Michaels and Ndeye Absa Gningue,** in a live webinar that will inspire and empower you. Whether you're a seasoned professional or just starting your journey, this event is tailored for anyone eager to enhance their leadership skills and make a real impact.

Register now and be part of this transformative experience!

www.womenwisdomnature.com